Lincoln and Kennedy: Redux

by G. Darrell Russell Jr.

DORRANCE
PUBLISHING CO
EST. 1920
PITTSBURGH, PENNSYLVANIA 15238

Dorrance Publishing Co
585 Alpha Drive
Pittsburgh, PA 15238
Visit our website at *www.dorrancebookstore.com*

ISBN: 979-8-89027-299-7
eISBN: 979-8-89027-797-8

LINCOLN AND KENNEDY: REDUX

A comparative look at the haunting aura of similarities of the personas and surrounding events affecting two U.S. presidents separated by one hundred years.

G. Darrell Russell Jr.

For my children, Eileen, Maureen, Graham, and Brendan, who have all wisely avoided careers in the political, legal, or public arenas.

Many thanks to my trusted, wise, and ever-patient paralegal, Nicole Warner, who has again suffered through the painful construction, with skilled fingers on the keys, of my latest modest project.

Previous Books by Author

Lincoln and Kennedy: Looked at Kindly Together (1972)
Hotbed for Hybrids: Lacrosse and Soccer in Baltimore (1978)
Chronicles from Court: In My Own Write (2004)
Commoner to Royalty: A Judicial Journal (2015)
Ten Hounds: A Personal Journal (2021)

CONTENTS

ONE: MARTYRDOM 1
"We do not know very much of the future except that
from generation to generation ..."

TWO: FAITH 17
"How many have been driven into outer darkness by
empty talk about faith...."

THREE: HUMOR 37
"There are three things which are real: God, human
folly and laughter..."

FOUR: POTPOURRI 55
"The tree the tempest with a crock of wood Throws
down in front of us..."

"Trust in the Lord with all your heart and lean not on your own understanding. In all your ways acknowledge Him. And He will make your paths straight."

3 Proverbs 5,6

FOREWORD

This paper was first produced by a young law student who eventually metamorphosed into a lawyer, who perhaps would have been better served to study court opinions in the law library, as opposed to pursuing a journalistic odyssey. A publisher was found, namely, Carlton Press of New York. And the words became a book entitled *Lincoln and Kennedy: Looked at Kindly Together.* The book never came close to the New York Times bestseller list. And eventually Carlton Press disappeared as the Ford Motor Company's Edsel. Over the years, I thought to myself, I would like to resurrect my youthful product and perhaps contemporize it. What you read in these pages is essentially my book, first published in 1973. Indeed, the words have a half century of accumulated dust. I did some tweaking but it's, alas, the same book.

Shortly after their deaths, Presidents Lincoln and Kennedy became martyrs and virtual saints in the mind of the public. Later, as tears dried, the essence of the myths could not be cut away. One part of the myth was the actual truth of striking similarities between the two martyrs. Similarities of circumstance, personality, and historical déjà vu. And a further composite of the myth was that both men, though flawed humans, were indisputably good men of a deep faith, with a twinkling eye for humor, and a somber awareness of tragedy. To wit, both lost young sons while living in the White House.

In addition to having been glorified by apotheosis, both men have been the victims of vilification during their lives and after. For instance, Kennedy was often characterized as a reckless raconteur whose wealthy family bought his elections and apologized for his character flaws. Lincoln was the back woods bumpkin who forced the U.S. into an unnecessary and horrific civil war. I make no pretentious historical judgments here. In the end, neither president lived long enough to fulfill their legacies and do all they wanted to do.

Indeed, there are striking parallels in the careers of these two assassinated presidents. Among the similarities are their premonitions of their impending deaths, their ignoring their aides' warnings not to make their fateful trips, their tenacious faith in the Lord, Jesus Christ, and their irrepressible wit. By way of emphasizing these similarities in chapter one, I employed italics for those parts of the texts which are repeated. That is, the same words are used to emphasize the similarities. It's almost as if Lincoln lived again in Kennedy - in principle, at any rate. I employed this literary trick to a lesser degree in chapter four.

I liberally filled the humor chapter with anecdotes, which were part of the persona of each man. They owned their jokes, and the jokes weren't cheap tales from the street corner or bar room. They were often just spontaneous remarks told with tongue in cheek. I tried to show the deep reservoir of faith of each president without proselytizing or sitting in on their confessionals. Chapter four includes all the surplusage similarities. I hope this still is of interest after the passage of half a century. Again, I am not presenting a historical treatise. And if you seek such, try Wikipedia!

AMDG

ONE: MARTYRDOM

"We do not know very much of the future except that from generation to generation the same things happen again and again." - T.S. Eliot

"You and I are together in the same fight as you saw me fighting before and, as you will have heard, I am fighting still..." - Philippians 1:30

The similarities between the tragic ordeals of the assassinations of Presidents Lincoln and Kennedy are extensive and disturbing. The similarities extend to their lives in relation to their deaths. Quite poignant was their haunting awareness of death. You could offer with validity that each followed a preordained plan of destiny which hurled them recklessly to their appointments with their tragic demise. The evidence is strong but might fail as a court proposition. But the coincidences are certainly intriguing.

The words following relate some of the similarities by way of narratives of Lincoln's and Kennedy's last days. Judge, if you wish, why these events repeat themselves. A court might rule that the evidence is all circumstantial. There is scant doubt that the events did repeat themselves. When words are italicized, they are the same in the Lincoln and Kennedy narratives. This is a writer's device to emphasize the parallels. I'm not really that clever. It's a simple evidentiary ploy to support the premise.

I may seem unduly critical of Richmond and Dallas and the South generally. This is by no means intentional. But it is a factual part of the dual accidents of fate. Lincoln and Kennedy could have been killed in Baltimore, Atlanta, or Memphis, each of which harbored pockets of antagonism. There could have been snipers in Boston or New York, for that matter. Senator Robert F. Kennedy was killed in Los Angeles, not a Southern city. But the two presidents were slain in southern meccas of hostility.

I have attempted to portray the respective calm before the storms of death. And then the storms before the calms, which calms Presidents Lincoln and Kennedy helped effect. Then the final explosive gusts of tornado like wind with streaks of lightning, which lashed out and felled the two leaders. This is a metaphor which could be developed ad nauseum. But the reader can conjure the possibilities. My case can never be fully proven, but circumstantial evidence is tantalizing.

TIME: April 14, 1865
PLACE: Washington, D. C.

Four chaotic, turbulent years had passed. The tall, melancholy figure in the White House had shouldered the burden of the bloody, American Civil War. The war was at last over and President Lincoln has finally been eased of his burden.

Five days earlier on Palm Sunday, General Ulysses S. Grant and General Robert E. Lee had met at the Appomattox Courthouse, situated in a suburb of Richmond. Lee, commander of all Confederate Armies, having been surrounded and faced with a hopeless situation, surrendered his army to Grant. (The remaining portion of the Confederate Army, surrendered to General Sherman on April 26,1865 at Hillsboro, North Carolina). News of Lee's surrender had reached

Washington toward the latter part of the day. At 4:30 PM, Grant sent official word via telegraph to the Secretary of War, E. M. Stanton: "General Lee surrendered the Army of Northern Virginia this afternoon on terms proposed by myself."

By nightfall, many in Washington knew of the glad tidings of Palm Sunday. And for those unaware, there could be no mistaking the message of booming cannons on the following morning. The flame of war would still burn in many hearts, and most would never forget; but the flame of violence had been doused. The crescendo of crashing guns and clanging swords had ceased.

The president's happiness was unmistakable as was that of the Washington citizenry; the people in the streets went exuberantly berserk. Everywhere crowds cheered, danced, got drunk, congratulated one another, shook hands with everyone, and then for want of other means of jollification, shook hands again.

These celebrations had begun eleven days ago when news of the fall of Richmond had reached Washington. And just when the celebration was beginning to wane, the news of Appomattox reached Washington. To be historically accurate, the U.S. Capital had been in a festive mood since April 3, 1865. It had been eleven bright, merry, buy your neighbor a drink, throw your hat in the sky days.

Lincoln had received word of the fall of Richmond while sojourning on the steamboat *Malvern*. He had set sail late in March for City Point, Virginia. His itinerary was to be close to the Union camps. He would visit Grant and his army in the field. He would visit the tents of the wounded of both armies. And he would include visits to the cities of Petersburg and Richmond on his southern tour.

The trip South was to be one of pleasure and relaxation, as well as business. Lincoln had earned and needed a vacation.

The president had been awaiting word of the fall of Richmond. And when it came, his relaxation began in earnest. Anxiety would invariably give way to contentment and peace. Appomattox would be anti-climactic; the only remaining fear was that Lee's army might escape. But this was not expected as they were a tattered, tired, and defeated army. Lincoln had determined to physically march his feet onto the soil of the city of Richmond.

Much anxiety and caution were expressed by Lincoln's inner circle about going south and entering the city of supposed enmity and hostility. Richmond was more than just a Southern city. It was a foreboding symbol; it represented more antagonism to Lincoln and his values than any other city. But the U.S. president boldly and bravely headed South.

The leading daily newspaper in Richmond termed Lincoln a coward, assassin, murderer, and fiend. Upon his arrival, crowds miraculously erupted from the crestfallen stillness of a vanquished city. At first predominately Negro, the phrases and cheers rang out: "Bless the Lord, there is the great Messiah!" Soon the streets came alive with white as well as black spectators. And while the whites were subdued, their relief at war's end could not be mistaken.

And of the Richmond citizenry, who allegedly had no use for Lincoln, who now lined the sidewalks and gazed from windows to ogle the procession in the streets, there appeared nothing overtly taunting or defiant in their faces. (This is the view of Admiral Porter of the *Malvern*. Lincoln's guard Crook interestingly observed less cordiality in those faces.) *Fatefully, however, it was a man who claimed Richmond citizenship who would perform one of history's most evil deeds.*

Lincoln's trusted guard, William Crook, observed a gun pointed directly at the president from a second story window. Crook stood in front of Lincoln and hid the tall target from a would-be assassin. Richmond and the South temporarily remained innocent of the impending crime, namely, the murder which would occur tonight.

Seeds of hatred for the Union North and its leader in the person of Lincoln were sown within John Wilkes Booth during his years in

Richmond. For this was the city where he scored his first dramatic success as an actor; where he was warmly befriended by the leaders of Southern society and politics; and where he briefly served as a member of Colonel Lee's Richmond Grays. The gun from the window was not Booth as he was in Boston at the time. However, when he learned that Lincoln had brazenly entered upon his beloved Richmond, Booth became enraged at himself for not going there and killing the president.

It was a triumphant day in Richmond. Journalist and eyewitness, L. P. Brockett, records his recollection of Lincoln that day: "Long anxious hours of care now seemed to be slipping from his shoulders, and brighter hours of hope and peace cast their radiance upon his heart and upon the future of his redeemed and beloved country."

The short stay in the South helped enkindle the warm end of the candle of life. It burned as brightly and gaily as ever. It was impervious to the ill wind blowing nearby which would soon snuff out the candle.

Lincoln left Richmond the same day and returned to his new boat. He had changed to the *River Queen* from the *Malvern* which was now taking his wife back to Washington. Four days later, the presidential craft, the *River Queen,* steamed from her moorings at City Point and headed for Washington. Almost immediately upon his arrival home, Lincoln learned of Appomattox.

And Washington's celebration continued. An eyewitness writes of that day when word of the victory became known: "In Washington, as in every town, and city in the loyal states, there was the wildest enthusiasm over the good news from the army. Flags were flying everywhere, cannons were sounding, business was suspended, and the people gave themselves to the impulse of joy and thanksgiving." (From the Lincoln biography by Francis F. Browne)

Thousands flocked to the White House lawn. Bands blared and played on, creating one of those scenes where a cacophony of noises is somehow pleasing to the ear. On April 10, 1865, Lincoln was forced to speak briefly, but after asking the band to play Dixie, he told everyone to come back tomorrow for what would be his last official speech.

The people who were to receive these words surely expected a speech of celebration, a speech of levity and good cheer, and a speech which would incite applause and hurrahs. However, the words were predominantly sober, reflective, and marked by subtle warning. He preferred speaking to the nation at this time not just to a cheering throng.

The president said, "By these recent successes the reinauguration of the national authority-reconstruction-which has had a large share of thought from the first, is pressed much more closely upon our attention. It is fraught with great difficulty and collaterals."

He used the analogy of the importance of one state to the well-being of the entire nation; each member of the body Union must be sound, lest the entire body suffer. Specifically, Louisiana had declared herself loyal to the Union and had adopted a favorable constitution. Lincoln thought it propitious that Louisiana be now accepted back into the Union without reprisal. He added, "What has been said of Louisiana will apply to other states."

Today, Friday, the skies are bright, the sun is warm, the cheering continues. In contrast, at the President's earlier and fatefully his last appearance, the air was filled with a fine mist, ominous and elusive. That was on April 11, when he spoke to the crowd from the White House balcony.

The president and his wife now prepare to go to the theatre. Lincoln is planning to attend mainly to please the large, still celebrating crowd, which is expected to attend, mainly to see the president. It had been well advertised that Lincoln would be present at Ford's Theatre this evening.

The president had earlier been discussing assassination with one of his trusted aides: "I know no one could do it and escape alive. But if it is to be done, it is impossible to prevent it." This conversation transpired often lately and most recently this afternoon with his guard, William Crook.

The president had always been conscious of death. He had recently had a frightening dream in which he discovered his lifeless body laid out in the East Room. *He had seen much death in war. He had witnessed much death in his family. He had lost a young son during his years in the White House. He had quoted a verse poignant with death,* from Shakespeare's *Macbeth.* (William Wallace Lincoln, called Willie, died in February 1862, of pneumonia. He was twelve years old.) "Duncan is in his grave. After life's fitful fever he sleeps well. Treason has done his worst. Nor steel, nor poison, can touch him further."

The president and his wife now embark for the theatre. As the carriage rumbles through the streets, the president tips his hat and waves to those who see him. On street corners and bar fronts, the crowds are still standing and cheering and celebrating.

At the theatre, now the play moves on sluggishly; it is mediocre at best, but the president finds it amusing. *The president having had much occasion to smile the last few days is smiling now.* Crack! *The air is split with the report of the murderer's gun. The lead ball penetrates the back of the president's head.*

Carl Sandburg writes:

> "For Abraham Lincoln it is lights out, good night, farewell and a long farewell to the good earth and its trees, its enjoyable companions and the Union of States and the world Family of Man he has loved. He is not dead yet. He is to linger in dying. But the living man can never again speak, see, hear, or awaken into conscious being."
>
> The scene is to crash and blare and flare as one of the wildest, one of the most inconceivable, fateful, and chaotic that ever stunned and shocked a world that heard the story.

Mrs. Lincoln springs for her husband and he falls in her lap. The guards shout, "Clear out!" And they carry the body across the street into the house of William Peterson.

Dr. Charles A. Leal soon pronounces, "His wound is mortal; it is impossible for him to recover."

The world soon utters, "Dear God, it can't be true!"

Secretary of the Navy Gideon Welles' first thoughts of the dying man stripped of his shirt are, "His large arms were of a size which one would scarce have expected."

Lincoln leaves us now. E. M. Stanton mutters the words: *"Now he belongs to the ages."*

ONE HUNDRED YEARS LATER
TIME: November 22, 1963
PLACE: Dallas, Texas

Almost three years had passed since the handsome young man from Boston had taken up residence in the White House. It had been turbulent for three years. But it had been a fruitful three years. Much had been done by this man of energy, brilliance and grace. The national purpose, the goals of a changing nation, the goals of the "New Frontier," all were becoming reality. New Frontier became the Kennedy campaign slogan.

The three years were marked by unprecedented economic growth as each month saw an increase in Gross National Product (GNP) and a decline in unemployment: a stemming of the tide of communism in the Western Hemisphere principally through the president's actions in the Cuban missile crisis; increased hemispheric cooperation through the Alliance for Progress; establishment of the Peace Corps; a thawing in the Cold War as evidenced by the nuclear test ban treaty; substantial progress in the case of Civil Rights; significant gains in the race to the moon; production of a plan of massive domestic legislation some of which has been passed and the remainder of which would hopefully soon be passed.

Indeed, much had been done. The beginning was now over. This is the day of mass automation, the day of instant travel and communications, the day of the computer. The day of social unrest, the day of unprecedented leisure, the day of the bomb. The vision of what must be done in the new day is now much clearer. We are truly living in a very different world.

One man had presciently seen that change was necessary; the nation had to get moving again. And he was witness to this growing need as early as 1940. The breakdown of many old ideas had then just begun. In his first book, *Why England Slept*, he astutely presented a great principle for public display: viz. that a totalitarian government can make people act and thus can perhaps be more effective in the short run particularly in military preparedness; however, a democracy has the responsibility of winning the people over before they will act; once this is accomplished, it functions more equitably and efficiently than any other system of modern government.

A new generation was now in command. A new image, a new leader had to win the people over and show them their new responsibilities. The public awakening was necessary first, then new motions could be made. The country was now truly moving again according to the plan of the New Frontier.

Though the skeptics were rapidly becoming believers, the remaining disbelievers were troublesome. And the hotbed of the vituperative antagonism of the disbelievers lay in the heartland of the Old South; an Old South that was very old indeed. The South didn't hear the voice which said, "this is a new age… we stand on the horizon of a new frontier… we must work together now… you can't do it alone anymore… all men really are created equal… take our hand and together we can work for the freedom and well-being of man."

The president was having quite a bit of trouble in Congress with the so-called Southern bloc. They were in large part responsible for the temporary hiatus of his program of domestic legislation and especially of his Civil Rights bill. The year 1964, an election year, was fast approaching and the Southern vote was a typical uncertainty. Thus, the first of several political visits to tour the South was planned for this weekend.

The president would fly to Texas and visit its leading cities. He would attempt to bring his charm directly to the voters while backstage he would attempt to bring peace between the feuding political leaders who had done so little to aid his program and whom he might need in '64. The feud was primarily between the governor and the senior U.S. senator. Vice President Johnson was from Texas. What better place to start the Southern excursions?

The trip South was to be one of pleasure and relaxation as well as business; Kennedy had earned and needed a vacation.

The president often said, "Let us begin." He so spoke in his inaugural address. Everything was "let us begin" or "take the first step... let's get moving again." Now the beginning of his administration with its goal and ideals was over. Relaxation was in order.

Air Force One, the presidential plane, had landed yesterday in San Antonio. Subsequent scheduled stops are Houston, Fort Worth, Dallas, and Austin. The climax of the trip is to occur tomorrow evening at the ranch of Vice President Johnson where elaborate festivities await the president and his party.

Today, this afternoon we are in Dallas. The arrival here was cause for considerable worry. Dallas had often been labeled as the "Southwest hate capital of Dixie."

Much anxiety was expressed among Kennedy's aides about entering this city of supposed enmity and hostility. Dallas was more than just a Southern city. It was a foreboding symbol; it represented more antagonism to Kennedy and what he stood for than any other place. But Kennedy went South without fear.

The cheering throngs at Love Airfield, from where the presidential party prepares to motor into Dallas, are making all fears seem baseless. The president has been facing challenges all his life; he is meeting this one and winning as usual. The motorcade begins and enters the city proper where the streets are lined up to ten deep. Windows are filled with smiling faces of welcome. The cheers are favorable.

And of this Dallas citizenry, who were supposed to have no use for Mr. Kennedy, and who now line the sidewalks and gaze from windows to watch the procession in the street, there appears nothing taunting or defiant in their faces. But it was a man who claimed Dallas citizenship who would perform one of history's most evil deeds.

Concern over this trip was not without good cause. One month earlier, the U.S. ambassador to the United Nations, Adlai E. Stevenson, had been jeered, jostled, and spat upon in Dallas. Vice President Johnson had been similarly maltreated here during the 1960 campaign. And earlier today and days prior to the gracious visit of President Kennedy, handbills bearing his picture and captioned "Wanted for Treason" were circulated. A full-page spread in the leading morning paper condemned the Kennedy administration with reckless abandon.

Arthur Schlesinger describes Dallas as a "city of violence and hysteria and its atmosphere was bound to affect people who were already weak, suggestible and themselves filled with chaos and hate." One person, a Lee Harvey Oswald, is now waiting in the Texas Book Depository building.

The crowds still cheer, The president smiles, waves alternately with his right, now his left hand.

Dallas gave President Kennedy his smallest vote among the big cities in 1960. But now suddenly that is hard to believe. Hugh Sidey of Time-Life publications says of today: "Texans jammed the sidewalks and spilled out into the street to see the president and his wife. It was still like a hundred cities all across the world that John

F. Kennedy had visited—curious, cheerful folk by the scores, by the thousands."

November was a favorite Kennedy month. The month of all his electoral victories, the month of his children's birthdays, the month of Yale vs. Harvard and Army vs. Navy, the month of Thanksgiving and the family reunion at Cape Cod. He was now happy at a welcome which seemed warm and sincere, and he was happy because it was November.

The short stay in the South helped enkindle the waxen end of his candle of life. It burned as brightly and gaily as ever. It was impervious to the ill wind blowing nearby which soon would snuff out the candle.

The president had prepared his speech soon to be delivered at the spacious Trade Mart towards which the motorcade inexorably moves. An elaborate luncheon in traditional Texas style, i.e., big, is awaiting the arrival of his party. Perhaps the president will give a stump-type speech–non-offensive, but entertaining and waxing rah, rah, vote Kennedy.

The people who were to receive these words surely expected a speech of celebration, a speech of levity and good cheer, and a speech which would incite applause and hurrahs. However, the words were predominantly sober, reflective, and marked by subtle warning. He preferred speaking to the nation this time, not just to a sheering throng.

Instead of speaking down to entertain the crowd, he wanted to speak out in a constructive fashion. Some of the words: "Ignorance and misinformation can handicap the progress of a city or company–but they can, if allowed to prevail in foreign policy, handicap this country's security. In a world of complex and continuing problems, in a world full of frustrations and irritations, America's leadership must be guided by the lights of learning and reason... this nation's strength and security are not easily or cheaply obtained–nor are they quickly and simply explained. There are many kids of strength and no one kind will suffice."

He used the analogy of the importance of one state to the well-being of the entire nation; each member of the body union must be sound lest the entire body suffer. Specifically, he wanted to show that Texas had been doing well despite a bad image which, sadly, had been ascribed to this state. He said: "In short, our national space effort represents a great gain in and a great resource of our national strength–and both Texas and Texans are contributing greatly to this strength." (This speech would never be delivered as he was murdered on his way to deliver it.)

Today, Friday, the skies are bright, the sun is warm, the cheering continues. In contrast, at the president's earlier and fatefully his last public appearance, the air was filled with a fine mist, ominous and elusive. That was in a parking lot in Fort Worth outside of his hotel.

President Kennedy had many more trips planned in the months ahead. He would want to visit hundreds of other American cities as well as many cities and towns in foreign lands. And this Texas trip is at the end of the beginning. That was over. He would continue with the comprehensive War on Poverty; there were hopes for successful passage of his Civil Rights bill, his tax act, his medical care for the aged bills. The Cold War was now a détente of wobbly peace and Southeast Asia had not yet become hot (but was rather warm). Actually, President Kennedy through diplomacy had averted several likely hot engagements which included Laos, Cambodia, Vietnam, the Congo, Cuba, and Berlin. Diplomacy was his forte. He was perhaps thinking of all these things now and optimistically smiling. The second term would be a terrific continuation.

The president had been earlier discussing assassination with some aides. "If anyone wants to do so, he can do it any day or night, if he is ready to exchange his life for mine." This conversation transpired often of late, and most recently this morning with Mrs. Kennedy and Kenny O'Donnell.

The president had always been conscious of death and particularly of dying young. *He had witnessed much death in his family. He had lost a young son during his years in the White House. He had quoted often a verse poignant with death* from John Buchanan's *Pilgrim's Way*. (Patrick Bouvier Kennedy died in August 1963,) "He loved his youth, and his youth has become eternal. Debonair and brilliant and brave, he is now part of that immortal England, which knows not age or weariness or defeat."

The presidential limousine and its entourage are now in downtown Dallas. From the Warren Commission Report: "In the downtown area, large crowds of spectators gave the president a tremendous reception. The crowds were so dense that special agent Clinton J. Hill had to leave the left front running board of the president's limousine... As the motorcade approached the intersection of Houston and Elm Streets, there was general gratification in the presidential party about the enthusiastic reception."

The president, having had much occasion to smile the last few days, is smiling now. Crack! *The air is split with the report of the murderer's gun. The lead ball penetrates the back of the president's head.*

To paraphrase Carl Sandburg:

> "For John F. Kennedy it is lights out, good night, farewell–and a long farewell to the good earth and its trees, its enjoyable companions, and the Union of States and the world Family of Man he has loved. He is not dead yet. He is to linger in dying. But the living man can never again speak, see, hear, or awaken into conscious being."
>
> ...The scene is to crash and blare and flare as one of the wildest, one of the most inconceivable, fateful, and chaotic that ever stunned and shocked a world that heard the story.

Mrs. Kennedy springs for her husband and he falls in her lap. The secret service men frantically shout to the driver of the president's car: "Let's get out of here." And they race with the limp body to Parkland Memorial Hospital.

Dr. Kemp Clark soon pronounces, "It's too late."

The world soon utters, "Dear God, it can't be true!"

Dr. Malcom Perry's first thoughts of the dying man stripped of his shirt are, "He's bigger than I thought he was."

Kennedy leaves us now.

Someone mutters the words: *"Now he belongs to the* ages."

TWO: FAITH

Dag Hammarskjold

The Apostles said to the Lord, "Increase our faith!"
And the Lord replied, "If you have faith the size of a mustard seed,
you could say to this mulberry tree,
'Be uprooted and planted in the sea,' and it would obey you."

Luke 17:5 , 6.

Thirty-six presidents have taken the same oath as prescribed by the Constitution of the United States: "I do solemnly swear (or affirm) that I will faithfully execute the office of president of the United States, and will to the best of my ability, preserve, protect, and defend the Constitution of the United States. *So, help me God."* (italics supplied)

The last four words are not a part of the official documents. But "So help me God" has been uttered by the president-elect at every inauguration. The founding fathers, the assembled delegates who authored the Constitution, took pains to keep separate church and state.

They added in Article VI of the Constitution: "...no religious test shall ever be required as a qualification to any office or public trust under the United States." But no chief executive has dared embark upon his voyage at the helm of the good ship Union, without a prayer for divine guidance.

The fathers did their work well. For truly there was a miracle at Philadelphia in the year 1787. Our Constitution has become the biblical rock upon which all the modern democracies have been built. Catherine Drinker Bowen in her work about this miracle writes: "The Federal Convention did not discuss religion. The relationship of church and state, already well established, was no part of its business. Yet there sat no delegate whose ideas of government or political philosophy were not profoundly influenced by his religious beliefs and training."

They argued that religion should be a personal affair. It follows that under such a system of government which places so much personal responsibility upon individuals, prayers can easily become passe. At times in the course of American history, loud and obnoxious voices would distort or completely reject those Western beliefs and traditions which have been so guardedly brought to America's shores.

Faith is the word; that's really what was brought to America. Vision and hope and courage, these too, but faith says it best, because it's so unchanging, yet so flexible.

The fathers knew our constitutional system must depend upon faith to work. That was as true yesterday as it is today. When our nation is healthy and at peace, the fragrant blossoms of American democracy pervade every part of the world; American faith is then strong. But ill winds of domestic or foreign strife can blow the blossoms to the ground; then, our faith is weak.

Every American can have an opinion in the affairs of his country, but no one can prove beyond a reasonable doubt that he has the answer. "There must be faith," says James Reston of *The New York Times*, "faith in our common purposes, faith in our religious and philosophic institutions, in our nation's politicism and in the men chosen to make and administer them." And the inspiration for this faith finds its best source in the person of the nation's leader.

It is to the lasting credit of the fathers that the Constitution seems to have bred, in this young country, many men of strong faith. John F. Kennedy and Abraham Lincoln were two such men. But events made their faith and their religion, as the ultimate expression of their faith, a pronounced part of their respective legends–more so than with any other president. When news of their shocking deaths reached the world, prayer was no longer passe. America learned to pray again. All peoples of the family of man bowed their heads in prayer. There was nothing else to do. Where else could one find solace in their grief?

Other presidents of the United States had died in office, but none of their deaths so stunned and shocked the world. The chief cause was that these two presidents had both died at the very peaks of their careers; they had just made a beginning of their work; and it was work of a timely nature done well so far. In their work they captured the imaginations of great numbers of varied peoples around the globe.

But it was the man himself, not the president, who had so affected the nation and the world; Lincoln, humble, simple in manner, strong, witty, mystically eloquent, honest and president during a tumultuous, crucial period, when his strength had appeared to have singly held the nation together. Kennedy youthful, witty, graceful, dashingly handsome, eloquent, and president during a crucial period of cold war and social flux, when his foresight and aplomb had appeared to have singly renewed national strength and vigor.

And suddenly they were gone. As people prayed, they hearkened to the fact that both were very good men, indeed men of faith, who had inspired a nation, each in his own unique manner. And their faith became a part of the Lincoln aura, the Kennedy aura. The pulpit became a forum to extol all their godly works and saintly deeds. They shortly became superhuman, faultless, and almost godlike. This was the myth.

But as tears dried and the objective historian began to pen his cool, unemotional analysis, a part of the myth could not be cut away. That is, both men were flawed but indisputably good men, men of deep and lasting faith. Perhaps this is why the myth continued.

THE FAITH OF LINCOLN

Science and technology have so remade the world today that it bears little resemblance to the world Lincoln knew one hundred fifty years ago. Science requires faith. The layman doesn't understand how a rocket can leap from earth and touch the moon and planets beyond. And what would today's citizens do without computers and cellphones. Man's mind has been endowed with endless potential.

These technological advances have deluded some and have helped reinforce an old theory; that is, man is all, man and the state! This is great! Faith is not a part of their credo. Such pomposity has merely lowered man's dignity by substituting self and state for the Western heritage of man's dependence upon a deity.

But such wonders and discoveries of this century are but a flicker next to man's greatest gift, the torch of life itself. This was the same torch that gave President Lincoln his basic simple faith more than one hundred fifty years ago, for imagine Abe Lincoln in Illinois:

> ...ambling with his long awkward gait over fresh green pastureland. The fields are full of lovely brown and white cows basking in the sunshine; they see the friendliness of Honest Abe's face and are unstirred by his approach. This is newly cut land and in the distance past the wheat fields are trees, hills, and more trees. A young

colt frolics in the penned stable area. Father Abraham wishes he could unloose the gate and give him more room to run and exert his freedom. The tall and gainly rail splitter approaches the farmhouse; the barnyard hens begin to chatter, the dog starts his greeting bark, the farmer comes out with extended hand, "Hi, neighbor. Did you walk all the way from Springfield?" Such were Lincoln's beloved farmlands of Illinois. It was a part of his faith. He watched young Tad Lincoln kneel at bedside and say: "Now I lay me down to sleep. I pray the Lord my soul to keep..." That was another part of his faith. Has the world changed very much?

Lincoln's secretary, biographer, John Hay, says of his president: "I consider Lincoln republicanism incarnate with all its faults and all its virtues. As, in spite of some rudeness, republicanism is the sole hope of a sick world, so Lincoln with all his foibles, is the greatest character since Christ." The words of the devoted Hay who was daily with Lincoln, in the later years, lend credence to the myth.

William Herndon, Lincoln's law partner for twenty-five years, writes of Lincoln:

> He lived in his thoughts and thought in his feelings. By these his soul was elevated and purified for his work. His work was the highest and grandest religion, noble duty, nobly done.
>
> Mr. Lincoln could be, and was, trusted by the people with almost omnipotent power, and he never abused it nor shook the public's faith in him. He was true to his trust, true to his country, and true to the rights of man. What a noble man, and what a noble life

he lived! Washington was America's creator. Lincoln was its savior. Mr. Lincoln now stands up against the deep, blue sky the grandest figure of his age.

I never knew so true a man, so good a one, so just a one, so uncorrupted and so incorruptible a one.

Take him all in all, he was as near a perfect man as God generally males.

Bishop Matthew Simpson of the Methodist Episcopal Church, in Washington D.C., said of Lincoln: "As a ruler, I doubt if any president has ever showed such trust in God, or in public documents so frequently referred to divine aid. Often did he remark to friends and delegations that his hope for our success rested in our conviction that God would bless our efforts, because we were trying to do right."

Another minister who had said to Lincoln that he "hoped the Lord was on our side," was greeted by an expected reply that it gave him no concern whether the Lord was on our side or not, "for" he added, "I know the Lord is always on the side of right." With feeling, Lincoln added, "but God is my witness that it is my constant anxiety and prayer that both myself and this nation should be on the Lord's side."

In the year before his death, Lincoln wrote to Josh Speed: "I am profitably engaged in reading the Bible. Take all of this book upon reason that you can and the balance upon faith and you will live and die a better man."

Sandburg writes: "Lincoln read the Bible closely, knew it from cover to cover, its famous texts, stories and psalms; he quoted it in talks to juries, in speeches, in letters."

Bosom friend of Lincoln, Senator Charles Sumner, observed Mrs. Lincoln assailing Jefferson Davis: "Do not allow him to escape the law—he must be hanged!" The president replied calmly, drawing on a lesson from the Sermon on the Mount, "Judge not, that ye not by judged." And when pressed again that the sight of Libby Prison made it impossible to pardon the Confederate chief, Lincoln repeated twice over the words, "Judge not, that ye not by judged." Lincoln used these same words in his second inaugural address.

He quoted the Bible in his acceptance speech of the Republican nomination of the United States Senate for the State of Illinois in June, 1858: "A house divided against itself cannot stand. I believe this government cannot endure permanently half-slave and half-free." He would use this phrase again and again, especially in the ensuing great debates with Senator Douglas (Chapter 4, *infra)*.

A man came complaining against his superior officer, rather loose-mouthed, and Lincoln merely told him to go home and read Proverbs 30:10, which read, "Accuse not a servant unto his master, lest he curse thee, and thou be found guilty."

Lincoln wrote a letter to his step-brother, John D. Johnston, concerning their dying father, "...tell him to remember to call upon, and confide in, our great and good, and merciful Maker, who will not turn away from him in any extremity. He notes the fall of a sparrow, and numbers the hairs of our heads; and he will not forget the dying man, who puts his trust in Him."

General Sickles, who had been wounded at Gettysburg, was visited at bedside by the president; he assured Sickles of success at Gettysburg. Upon Sickle's query as to the reason for Lincoln's confidence, the latter answered:

> When Lee crossed the Potomac and entered Pennsylvania followed by our Army, I felt the crisis had come. I knew that defeat in a great battle on northern soil involved the loss of Washington, to be followed, perhaps, by the intervention of England and France in

favor of the Southern Confederacy. I went to my room and got down on my knees in prayer. Never before had I prayed with so much earnestness. I wish I could repeat my prayer. I felt that I must put all my trust in Almighty God. He gave our people the best country ever to man. He alone could save it from destruction. I had tried my best to do my duty and found myself unequal to the task. The burden was more than I could bear. God had been our protector in other days. I prayed that he would not let the nation perish. I asked him to help us and give us victory now.

Lincoln felt that his prayer was answered. Thank you Jesus.

Most of Lincoln's intimates saw him as having piety and spiritual resources, but more subdued about his religion, than General Sickles represented. But among those close to him, respect and loyalty was total. Secretary Seward said, "The president is the best of us."

Henry J. Raymond, of *The New York Times*, wrote in his diary of a conversation with Seward: "Of President Lincoln he spoke in the strongest terms of praise. With all his defects, he said, he seemed just the man for the crisis. Patient, capable of endurance, just and tolerant beyond example, he said that Providence had raised him up for this emergency as signally as he raised up Washington for the necessities of our struggle for independence."

Historian William E. Barton writes: "Lincoln not only had faith in prayer considered as a means of obtaining results from God; he believed in it as establishing a relation with God, a covenant relation such as Abraham of old established."

Emmanuel Hertz lecturing before the Forum of the Jewish Center said of Lincoln: "This man's whole life was one long fervent prayer that the eyes of his fellow men be opened to their humane duty of treating their fellow men with fairness, to do justice, to love mercy, and walk humbly with their creator."

The president's faith in God and country radiates like the bright sun from the words of his Springfield farewell:

> No one not in my position can appreciate the sadness I feel at the parting. To these people I owe all I am. Here I have lived for more than a quarter of a century; here my children were born, and here one of them is buried. I know not how soon I shall see you again. A duty devolves upon me which is, perhaps, greater than that which has devolved upon any other man since Washington. He would never have succeeded except for the aid of Divine Providence, upon whom he at all times relied. I feel that I cannot succeed without the same Divine aid which sustained him, and on the same Almighty Being I place my reliance and support; and I hope you, my friends, will all pray that I may receive that Divine assistance, without which I cannot succeed, but with which success is certain. Again, I bid you all an affectionate farewell.

Humility came from his faith. To Noah Brooks, he once said, "I am sure that if I do not go away from here a wiser man, I shall go away a better man, for having learned here what a very poor sort of man I am."

And honestly, patience and courage. Only such a strong courageous man could have shouldered a burden such as Lincoln did, and yet remain so steady and cool. He was so cool that Horace Greeley, of the *New York Tribune*, mistook this virtue and thought that Lincoln was too bland and easygoing.

Secretary Cameron had received a formal record of censure from Congress. Lincoln courageously sent a message to the Senate and House: "Congress will see that I should be wanting equally in candor and in justice if I should have the censure expressed in this resolution to rest exclusively or chiefly upon Mr. Cameron... It is due to Mr. Cameron to say that, although he fully approved the proceedings, they were not moved nor suggested by himself and that not only the president, but all other heads of departments were at least equally responsible with him for whatever error, wrong, or fault was committed in this premises."

Nicolay and Hay noted that Cameron gratefully remembered this voluntary and manly defense of his official integrity.

Lincoln addressed an audience in New York City several months before the '60 election: "Let us have faith that right makes might, and in that faith, let us, to the end, dare to do our duty as we understand it."

Harpers Weekly commented on a drawing of Lincoln presented to its readers shortly after the Republican Convention in Baltimore. "...Through an infinite perplexity of events the faith of the president has never faltered... Look thoughtfully at his rugged face. In its candor, its sagacity, its calmness, its steadiness, and strength, there is especially conspicuous the distinctive American."

Noah Brooks quoted Lincoln as saying to him: "I should be the verist shallow and self-conceited blockhead upon this footstool if in my discharge of the duties which are put upon me in this place, I should hope to get along without the wisdom that comes from God and not from men."

Lincoln had deep religious convictions at the root of his faith. He was a legend's hero. These facts are real. Was he a saint? Maybe. Part of the sainthood myth began with those colored folk set free by Lincoln. A white-haired Negro was heard to ask, "What do you know 'bout Massa Linkum?' And the answer, "Massa Linkum be everywhere. He walk de earth like de Lord." He was their mystic hero (Chapter 4, *infra.*); their reverence bordered on superstation. "God bless Massa Linkum!" "De Lawd save Fader Abraham!"

Compassion was a part of his faith. Upon granting one of hundreds of pardons to the Confederate husband of a pleading wife, the latter broke into tears. Lincoln reproached her: "My dear woman, if I had known how badly it was going to make you feel, I never would have pardoned him." "You don't understand me." She cried between sobs. "Yes, yes, I do. And if you don't go away at once, I shall be crying with you."

Charity was a part of his faith. In an informal speech shortly after his second election, his heart throbbed with mercy towards the separated American brethren: "So long as I have been here, I have not willingly planted a thorn in any man's bosom... I have striven and shall strive to avoid placing any obstacle in the way..." For he knew well the scriptural lesson of Matthew 18 which admonishes against causing another's stumbling. He was the classic practitioner of the adage: "Love thy neighbor as thyself."

Lincoln was unorthodox in the practice of his Christian faith. He did not adhere to any strict Christian dogma and did not possess formal membership in any one particular church. For these reasons, some members of the clergy had opposed his candidacy. He was moved to this explanation of his religious tenets:

> I know there is a God and that He hates injustice and slavery. I see the storm coming and I know that His Hand is in it. If He has a place and work for me, and I think He has, I believe that I am ready.

THE FAITH OF KENNEDY

One hundred years later, some of President Lincoln's problems still remain. These, plus the new challenges of an ostensibly different world, have made the president's job very complex. But he has understood the issues, defined them and met them head on. Sandburg was quoted as saying: "The way he [Kennedy] is doing is almost too good to be true. There has never been a more formidable set of historical conditions for a president to face since Lincoln."

Kennedy brought an exceptionally keen understanding of the world to Washington as a young congressman. His vision was perhaps first noticeable in his book, *Why England Slept*, published more than eighty years ago (Chapter One, *supra*). He was giving harbingers of warning to America that they "not be lulled by the momentary calm of the sea, or the somewhat clearer skies above." This lesson is still true today. At the beginning of his third year, he would say to the nation; "...we welcome those winds... we have every reason to believe our tide is running strong."

President Kennedy understood the changing world because his faith gave him the insight to see those basic truths which time never changes; He knew well the scriptural lesson from Ecclesiastes: "There is nothing new under the sun." And he knew the torch of life itself was the greatest twentieth century phenomenon. This gave him the same basic faith that it had given Abraham Lincoln one hundred years earlier, for imagine Jack Kennedy in Massachusetts:

> ...strolling along the white sandy beach of Hyannisport. He takes quick medium-length strides, fingers in and thumbs out of pockets, sort of holding on to pocket's edge which leaves the elbows suspended at angle bent slightly backward, like wings. The head is tilted forward. His shoulders are shrugged up giving just a hint

of squareness. He effuses a picture of determined forward motion. A school of porpoises curiously bobs in
and out of the water not far from the shore; perhaps they
sense his intriguing presence. He looks up at a gentle
formation of white geese and smiles. A noisy brown fox
terrier scurries close behind stopping, then running to
catch master Jack. The dog's excited, disorganized gait
leaves sand flying in four different directions.

This was the Kennedy compound during summer
in Massachusetts. It was part of his faith.

He watched young John-John Kennedy kneel at
bedside and say, "Now I lay me down to sleep. I pray
the Lord my soul to keep." That was another part of
his faith. The world really hasn't changed that much.

His religion as the ultimate expression of his faith was perhaps best understood by his long-time friend, the late Richard Cardinal Cushing,
Archbishop of Boston. The good cardinal was a familiar face around
the Kennedys for as long as one could remember.

The cardinal reflected:

> I don't think the late president would want me to say
> that he was a very religious man. As a matter of fact, I
> wouldn't want anybody to say that I was a very religious
> man, because I was sort of a natural type... (but) Ken-
> nedy, since he became president, had become a pray-
> erful man. I know that after he assumed the office of
> president of the United States, he had many sleepless
> nights, and during those periods of sleepless hours, he
> would get up out of his bed and kneel down and pray. I
> think that we had a president with one hand in the hand

of God–but for some reason, God permitted him to be
taken from us.

The cardinal, on another occasion, wrote that Kennedy was "a man of strong religious commitments... his grace of style, his boundless courage, his patient suffering, his self-assurance, and the warmth of his affection–all these were rooted in a faith that was anchored beyond this world, truly in God Himself."

The fact that Kennedy was the first Roman Catholic elected to the presidency plays no small part in his share of the Lincoln-Kennedy sainthood myth. American Catholics, numbering some forty million, and millions of other Catholics around the globe, assumed that two saints here lived during their lives, namely, Pope John XXIII and President Kennedy. There is a very cogent analogy in that they were each, at the same point in history, liberal revolutionaries within their religious and secular spheres. There's the rub. The two spheres have become confused and undistinguishable.

John Kennedy was uniquely required to declare his faith before his fellow citizens and to defend it publicly.

From a Kennedy campaign speech: "...if this election is decided on the basis that forty million Americans lost their chance of being president on the day they were baptized, then it is the whole nation that will be the loser."

Because Kennedy defended his faith so well, he earned the respect of men of good will everywhere, and many suspicions were dissipated, and many ancient prejudices were erased.

Arthur M. Schlesinger, Jr., special presidential assistant, with a daily observation point in the White House, indicates that the president possessed a more acute secular mind than theological mind, writing: "He assimilated a good deal of the structure of the Catholic faith, encouraged probably by his mother and sisters. He often adopted the Catholic side in historical controversy, as in the case of Mary, Queen of Scots; and he showed a certain weakness for Catholic words of art, like 'prudence,' and a certain aversion toward bad words for Catholics, like 'liberal.' He felt an immense sense of fellowship with Pope John XXIII." Schlesinger feels that Kennedy's example helped create the progressive and questing American Catholicism of the sixties.

Theodore C. Sorensen, Kennedy's close advisor and assistant for more than a decade, gives his impression of the Kennedy religion: "He did not believe that all virtue resided in the Catholic Church, nor did he believe that all Catholics would (or should) go to heaven. He felt neither self-conscious, nor superior about his religion... he faithfully attended Mass on Sunday, even in the midst of fatiguing out of state travels when no voter would know whether he attended services or not."

Sorensen relates an early conversation where Kennedy told him, "There is an old saying in Boston that we get our religion from Rome and our politics at home." And in a letter from Kennedy: "There is nothing inconsistent about believing in the separation of church and state and being a good Catholic–quite the reverse... I don't believe there is... [any] conflict between being a Catholic and fulfilling your constitutional duties."

Sorensen feels that all the Kennedy boys inherited much of their shy but appealing warmth and spiritual depth from their mother, Mrs. Rose Kennedy. Mrs. Kennedy must have been well pleased to receive a letter from thirteen-year-old Jack attending his only year at parochial school, the Canterbury School in New Milford, Connecticut: "We have chapel every morning and evening, and I will be quite pious I guess when I get home." Upon transferring to non-denominational Choate, the following year, he kept his religious habits, writing his mother, "I received Communion this morning and am going to church on Tuesday." Mrs. Kennedy relates that she had a "wonderfully happy feeling to see Jack start his new Administration with Mass in the morning.: He still possessed those religious habits of his youth.

Mr. Joe Kennedy's contribution consisted in chief with imbuing Jack with a sense of direction and responsibility. He wrote Jack at school with a subtle chastisement for a poor grade in penmanship: "After long experience in sizing up people, I definitely know you have the goods and can go a long way. Now aren't you foolish not to get all there is out of what God has given you..."

From early in his political career his Catholicism helped attract attention to him as well as contributing to the Kennedy sainthood myth after his death. Schlesinger told Joe McCarthy, biographer of the Kennedy family, "Jack's Catholicism is the very thing that has brought him into prominence. Looking as Jack does and talking as he does, a liberal-minded senator from New England, who went to Choate School and comes from a wealthy family–if he were just another Protestant, nobody would pay much attention to him.

As early as 1950, Congressman Kennedy was addressing the graduates at Notre Dame. "You have been taught that each individual has an immortal soul, composed of an intellect which can know truth and a will which is free. Because of this every Catholic must believe in the essential dignity of the human personality on which any democracy must rest."

Kennedy readily and proudly admits to the source of his faith. He said in New Ross, Ireland, in the summer of 1963: "When my great-grandfather left here to be a cooper in East Boston, he carried nothing with him except two things: a strong religious faith and a strong desire for liberty. I am glad to say that all his great-grandchildren have valued that inheritance."

Senator Kennedy answered a constituent's inquiry as to whether he had attended parochial school: "...neither my brother Joe nor I attended a parochial school. My brothers Bob and Ted did, however, and so did my four sisters... What is important in this particular regard is whether you hold to the tenets of your faith. I do and so do the other members of my family."

The Canadian Parliament on May 1961 heard him attempt to put new vigor in the faith of two countries: "This trip is more than a consultation–more than a good-will visit. It is an act of faith–faith in your country, in your leaders–faith in the capacity of two great neighbors to meet their common problems–and faith in the cause of freedom, in which we are so intimately associated."

A man with faith is irrevocably drawn toward religion as the supreme expression thereof. The truly good man is a man of deep faith and religion–as Kennedy–as Lincoln. But courage is also a part of the mixture.

Kennedy said in his Pulitzer Prize-winning *Profiles in Courage:*

> A man does what he must–in spite of personal consequences, in spite of obstacles and dangers and pressures...each one's need to maintain his own respect for himself was more important to him than his popularity with others–because his desire to win or maintain a reputation for integrity and courage was stronger than his desire to maintain his office–because his conscience, his personal standard of ethics, his integrity or morality–call it what you will–was stronger than the pressures of public disapproval–because his faith that his course was the best one, and would ultimately be vindicated, outweighed his fear of public reprisal.

The late Dr. Martin Luther King, Jr. reflected: "He had the vision and wisdom to see a problem in all its dimensions, and the courage to do something about it."

Former Secretary of Defense Robert McNamara, said: "He had wit and humor and style, yes, and with it all he had a more important capacity–moral and ethical insight."

As a freshman senator, he personally answered a letter from a young girl, who as a member of a teenage Youth Fellowship, was inquiring what prayer meant to him. He answered:

> I believe that man is created by God with an immortal soul. I believe that those who follow His teaching will be rewarded by eternal life with Him in Heaven. On the long and difficult road of life, it is quite natural that we should turn to Him, our Master, for guidance and for relief from troubles that beset us. It is unfortunate that too often we are prone to turn to Him only in moments of difficulty, but He never permits prayers to go unanswered.
>
> When my crew and I were lost for several days in the last days in the last war, after being shipwrecked, I believe that the prayers were directly responsible for us finally being rescued. This is only one example of when prayer has been of assistance to me. In short, prayer can help all of us, both individually and as a Nation in the difficult days ahead.

Just as courage was a part of his faith, so were gentleness and charity. Charles Bartlett says that Kennedy never gossiped about anyone "and when somebody else did it, he was impatient; he didn't like to hear sharp words about anyone. This gentleness is something that I don't think was fully appreciated about John Kennedy."

Cardinal Cushing says Kennedy's favorite scriptural passages were almost uniformly those that emphasized courage, and home, and confidence in God.

From a dedication breakfast of International Christian Leadership, Inc.... "Every president has taken comfort when told... that the Lord will be with thee. He will not fail thee nor forsake thee. Fear not–neither be thou dismayed."

Before the General Assembly of the United Nations: "But man does not live by bread alone and the members of the organization are committed by the charter to promote and respect human rights."

Before the United States Chamber of Commerce: "But the Bible tells us that there is a time for every purpose under the heaven... a time to cast away stones and a time to gather stones together. And, ladies and gentlemen, I believe it is time for us all to gather stones together to build this country as it must be built in the coming years."

In the Houston Coliseum during the presidential Campaign: "For the making of peace is the noblest worth of God-fearing men. It is the righteous way. And righteousness exalteth a nation."

Evelyn Lincoln, Kennedy's personal secretary, writes that seeing her president labor though a stormy week and then drive off to Mass on Sunday morning reminded her of the old adage, "God helps those who help themselves."

Kennedy often used the following words in speeches. Evelyn Lincoln once found them hidden on a slip of paper among some classified material. She remarked only that the words Kennedy had scribbled "were curious and the language almost poetic":

> I know there is a God–and I see a storm coming; if he
> has a place for me, I believe that I am ready.

THREE: HUMOR

Those who thrust themselves into the political arena are always faced with the necessity, at one time or another, of reaching into their bag of jokes to stimulate their audience. This bag is standard equipment in the political trade. Most of our presidents brought this equipment to the White house, or writers with the equipment. But two presidents had such a deep bag of jokes that their flair for the humorous became an inextricable part of their image. And later, part of a legend.

President Lincoln was the first real humorist to occupy the White House and President Kennedy was the second. They each were recognized everywhere as having a genuine gift for provoking laughter. They had a relish for satire, a knack of needling others as well as themselves, an impulse for the comic, and a deep appreciation of the value of good humor.

Their laughter was infectious. The mood of the entire nation was affected. The sixties of the nineteenth and twentieth centuries were marked by a rebirth of satire with two presidents being the center and cause. They were terrific jokesters so people felt at ease to joke about them first and then about everything else that other people in a different place and/or different time might think too serious to joke about.

Americans are by nature irreverent; the nation boasts of a long line of eminent artists and writers who make their chief claim to prominence through their satirical works. But twice a phenomenon of sorts occurred; the natural flow of wit from the White House set the inherent American irreverence ablaze.

Sandburg explains the phenomenon of the 1860s: "Pomp and power would drop into collapse and shuffle with a limping dignity if looked at long enough." Some of those who looked long enough were Artemus Ward, Orpheus Kerr, Petroleum Vesuvius Nasby, David R. Locke, etc. Newspapers and periodicals were filled with their work and that of others. A stream of publications flooded the stands such as *Abe Lincoln's Jokes, Mr. Lincoln's Funny Bone, Abe Lincoln: Anecdotes and Stories, Old Abe's Jokes Fresh from Abraham's Bosom, Abe Lincoln: Yarns and Stories,* and others. They offered Lincoln humor and poked fun too. It was all rather clever and sometimes rollickingly funny.

Artemus Ward wrote this well-circulated, very typical bit, containing a mock interview with Lincoln:

I called on Abe. He received me kindly. I handed him my umbreller and told him I'd have a check for it if he pleased. "That," sed he, "puts me in mind of a little story. There was a man out in our parts who was so mean that he took his wife's coffin out of the back winder for fear he would rub the paint off the doorway. Wall, about this time there was a man in an adjacent town who has a green cotton umbreller."

"Did it fit him well? Was it custom made? Was he measured for it?"

"Measured for what?" sed Abe.

"The umbreller?"

"Wall, as I was saying," continued the president, treatin the interruption with apparent contempt, "this man sed he'd know that there umbreller ever since it was a parasol. Ha, ha, ha!"

"Yes," sed I, larfin in a respectful manner, "but what has this man with the umbreller to do with the man who took his wife's coffin out of the back winder?"

"To be sure," sed Abe–what was it? I must have got two stories mixed together, which puts me in mind of another lit–" etc. *(Laughter.)*

Schlesinger explains the phenomenon of the 1960s. "For Kennedy wit was the natural response to platitude and pomposity." And for others, too. Political satirists once again could stab at platitude and pomposity without noticeable restraint. The leaders, Murry Kempton, Bernard Levin, Russell Baker, Al Capp, Art Buchwald to name a few, found new avenues to explore and new prominence. All the newsstands were flooded with publications centering on Kennedy humor, something that hadn't happened for one hundred years. To name a few: *The Kennedy Wit, The New Frontier Joke Book, The Humor of JFK, See Jack Run, More Kennedy Wit*, etc.

Perhaps the most circulated satire of all was the record Album "The First Family." To paraphrase a scene from the record:

> Bobby Kennedy confronts his brother the president: "I would like to discuss yesterday's touch football game with you. Now on three different occasions I was tackled–once by Senator Dirksen, once by Senator Goldwater, and once by Mr. Hoffa. Now as attorney general I can tell you that a tackle in touch football is illegal and you should have called a penalty."
>
> The president answers, "Yes, Bob, you are the attorney general, but when you play here you play by my rules, or you don't play at all. And I guess you know why."
>
> Bobby: "Why?"
>
> Jack: "Because it's my ball, that's why!" (*Laughter*)

THE HUMOR OF LINCOLN

Abraham Lincoln probably developed his funny bone at a very early age. Reading and re-reading *Pilgrims Way* and *Aesop's Fables*, he assimilated the beauty and art of storytelling. As a young attorney, riding the circuit in his native Illinois, he shared many evenings with his fellow members of the bar and distinguished judges, trading stories in the rude taverns which were then one of the few social outlets of frontier life.

Alexander K. McClure, of the Philadelphia *Times*, says of those formative years of the Lincoln humor:

"The Western people thus thrown together with but limited sources of culture and enjoyment, logically cultivated the storyteller, and Lincoln proved to be the most accomplished in that line of all the members of the Illinois bar."

Mr. McClure, an editor and Lincoln's closest friend among the press, also says:

"I have never in all my intercourse with public men, known one who was so apt in humorous illustration as Mr. Lincoln, and I have known him many times to silence controversy by a humorous story with pointed application to the issue."

Isaac Arnold conveys the initial impression of an encounter with Lincoln:

"If he spoke, before many words were uttered, the hearer would be impressed with his clear, direct good sense, his simple homely short Anglo Saxon words, and by his wonderful wit and humor."

It was never reckless humor nor disrespectful. It was nearly always controlled, cool, and purposeful. And it was never harsh or vulgar. McClure adds that "none despised vulgarity more than Lincoln." And Frank Carpenter, White House artist-painter, could not recollect a single Lincoln story "which would have been out of place in a ladies' drawing room."

David R. Locke, a leading satirist of the day, expresses deep admiration for a fellow tradesman:

"Mr. Lincoln's flow of humor was a sparkling spring, gushing out of a rock–the flashing water had a somber background which made it all the brighter."

General James B. Fry relates: "Mr. Lincoln's wit and mirth will give him a passport to the thoughts and hearts of millions who would take no interest in the sterner and more practiced part of his character."

And a Colonel James S. Brisling rated Lincoln as "undoubtedly the champion joker of the United States."

The *Saturday Review* of London observed with interest the new nation across the ocean, deeply enmeshed in the fratricidal war and yet finding time to laugh without noticeable restraint: "We never treated lightly our Indian mutiny, nor did our forefathers ever laugh at the great colonial revolt; but then we have not the Yankee *esprit*, nor the recklessness which is its root. One advantage which the Americans now have in national joking is the possession of a president who is not only the First Magistrate, but the Chief Joker of the Land."

Arnold contrasts the unfailing humor of Lincoln with the burden of his office: "Mirthfulness and melancholy, hilarity and sadness, were strongly combined in him. His mirth was sometimes exuberant. It sparkled in jest, story and anecdote" to be suddenly followed with sadness as he perhaps was drawn to the sounds of crashing rifles, always nearby.

Ward Lamon corroborates Arnold, saying that Lincoln used stories as a laugh cure for his own melancholy; but he also used them for a drooping friend or to clinch an argument, to disarm an antagonist or to lay bare a fallacy.

Lincoln's humor inevitably became associated with his name and personality. It was always a part of him; it most frequently gushed out in the form of a story.

When Lincoln was writing the Emancipation Proclamation, he asked Secretary of State Seward for suggestions. Seward recommended a change of a word. A few minutes later Seward suggested another minor change. Lincoln asked him why he hadn't proposed both of his important changes at once. Seward hedged. Lincoln began his story saying that Seward reminded him of a hired man out West who came to the farmer one afternoon with news that one of a yoke of oxen had dropped dead. And after hesitation and waiting a while, the hired man said the other ox in the team had dropped dead too. The farmer asked, "Why didn't you tell me at once both oxen were dead?" "Because", said the hired man, "I didn't want to hurt you by telling you too much bad news at one time."

Near the end of the war when the Confederate forces were about to surrender, Lincoln was asked what he intended to do with Robert E. Lee after he was captured.

"Well," he began, "I remember a boy I used to know back in Springfield who saved his money and bought a raccoon. The novelty of having this coon soon wore off and the boy got tired of him. One day he was leading the coon through the streets on the end of a rope, and he had his hands full to keep clear of the little coon who had bitten him and torn his clothes. At last, he sat down on a curbstone with his face as long and as grim as mine usually is when I sit for a portrait. A man passing by asked the lad what the matter was.

"'Oh,' said the lad, 'this coon's such a trouble to me!"

"'Why don't you get rid of him then?' asked the sympathizer.

"'Sh-sh,' said the boy, 'I'm letting him claw through his rope so I can tell folks he got away!'" *(Laughter)*

A delegation of preachers called on Lincoln and offered advice which they assured him was the Lord's will.

"Well, gentlemen!" began the retort. "It is not often that I am honored by a delegation direct from the Almighty!"

The presence of the eminent ministers provided occasion for another yarn:

"Down in New Orleans before the war there was a chap who went up on a balloon. He was all decked out in fine silks and spangles like a fairy prince. Off he floated in his basket, and several hours later landed in a cotton field where some darkies were working. One look at him and they ran off like rabbits all except one white-haired old fellow who was too rheumatic to run. He just stood still, removed his hat and bowed low as the dazzling balloonist stepped out of his basket.

"'Good morning, Massa Jesus!' he said, 'How's you pa?" *(Laughter)*

Lincoln would wax satirical if the occasion presented itself. One such occasion arose shortly after the '48 Democratic Convention had nominated General Cass. The Democrats were zealously attempting to imbue Cass with a military reputation in the traditional Old Hickory image. Lincoln, then a congressman, rose from his seat in the House to give his views on their efforts:

"Yes, sir all his biographers [Cass's], and they are legion, have him in hand, tying him to a military tail, like so many mischievous boys tying a dog to a bladder of beans. [*Laughter*]... He was not at Hull's surrender, but he was close by; he was a volunteer aide to General Harrison... and... was 'aiding' Harrison to pick huckleberries. *(Laughter)*

"By the way, Mr. Speaker, did you know I am a military hero? Yes, sir, in the days of the Black Hawk war, I fought, bled, and came away. Speaking of General Cass's career reminds me of my own. I was not at Stillman's defeat, but I was about as near as Cass was to

Hull's surrender; and like him I saw the place very soon afterwards. It is quite certain I did not break my sword, for I had none to break; but I bent a musket pretty badly on one occasion. [*Laughter*], and although I never fainted from loss of blood, I can truly say I was often very hungry." [*Laughter*]

Lincoln's humor could be a tidy rejoinder. After a scolding from Lincoln for not sending more complete reports, General McClellan sent the president this telegram: "Have captured two cows. What disposition should I make of them?" And the president, "Milk 'em, George."

Lincoln attributed McClellan's indecisiveness during the was as being a case of the "slows."

A tale of the "slows": While General McClellan was "resting" his troops, the president was asked what number of men the Southern forces had in the field. Lincoln answered, "1,200,000 according to the best authority." When this ghostly figure brought disbelief to the questioner, Lincoln continued, "Yes sir —1,200,000–no doubt about it. You see, all our generals, when they get whipped, say the enemy outnumbers them from three to five to one, and I must believe them. We have 400,000 in the field, and three times four makes twelve. Don't you see it?"

From a '60 campaign speech in Connecticut: "I am reminded of the man who had a poor old lean, bony spavined horse, with swelled legs. He was asked what he was going to do with such a miserable beast– the poor creature would die. 'Do?' said he. 'I am going to fatten him up; don't you see that I have him fat as high as the knees?' [*Laughter*] Well, they've got the union dissolved up to the ankle but no farther." *(Laughter and applause)*

From a later speech: "I have come to see you and allow you to see me and insofar as the ladies, I have the best of the bargain on my side. I don't make that acknowledgement to the gentlemen." *(Laughter)*

His humor could be spontaneous. Jay Cooke, financier and U.S. subscription agent; Secretary of the Treasury Chase; Attorney General Bates, and the president drove out to a drill review seven miles beyond Georgetown. Cooke got to looking at the back of Bates' head as the carriage leisurely moved along. He noticed that Bates' hair was black, but his whickers and mustache were white. Cooke wondered aloud why this was so. Lincoln gave a quizzical look at Bates and spoke. "Oh, Mr. Cooke, that is easily accounted for. The cause is that he uses his jaws more than he does his brain."

Lincoln addressed Sherman's troops, offering to hear any grievance. An officer stepped forward saying, "Mr. President, this morning I went to speak to Colonel Sherman, and he threatened to shoot me." Lincoln stepped forward, and in a stage whisper, audible to everyone in the outfit, said to the officer, "Well, if I were you and he threatened to shoot, I would not trust him, for I believe he would do it." The officer flushed and disappeared. The troops whooped.

And to an aide who was attempting to favorably compare King Charles I bargain with the armed forces who were making war on his government and the suggestion of Lincoln's bargaining with the rebels: "My only distinct recollect of the matter is that Charles lost his head."

About his feverish but sometimes intractable secretary of war, Lincoln intoned: "We may have to treat him as they are sometimes obliged to treat a Methodist minister I know of out West. He gets wrought up to so high a pitch of excitement in his prayers and exhortations, that they are obliged to put bricks in his pockets to keep him down. We may be obliged to serve Stanton in the same way, but I guess we'll let him jump awhile first." (*Laughter*)

To one asking whether the town of Lincoln, Illinois, was named after him, Lincoln replied with gravity, "Well, it was named after I was." (*Laughter*)

And to a gunnery mate on a mortar vessel who said to the president, "I have the right elevation and can land a shell on the dome of the capitol. Sir, if you wish." Lincoln smiling, "No, leave it where it is. That is the best place for it." (*Laughter*)

Ralph Waldo Emerson wrote of Lincoln: "He is the true history of the American people of his time." Because Lincoln could still smile in the face of adversity, the people could too. They smiled less after he had gone. (*Laughter fades*)

THE HUMOR OF KENNEDY

President Kennedy's gift for wit began at an early age; it undoubtedly arose from a happy and secure family environment. During the early years he was recognized as an ace prankster (e.g., swiping the chocolate frosting from brother Joe's plate), given to witty phrases ("Before I would spend 20 cents of my 40-cent allowance and in five minutes I would have empty pockets and nothing to gain and 20 cents to lose") and a constant source of levity.

His teacher at the Choate school wrote to the senior Mr. Kennedy ascribing to Jack a talent for "witty expression" and "natural cleverness." But the teacher, George St. John, added that Jack had yet to learn "the right place for humor." This same teacher many years later reminisced about young Jack: "...he had a delightful sense of humor, always... in any school, he would have got away with some things, just on his smile. He was a very likeable person very lovable."

Understatement and satire were not late refinements of Kennedy wit but showed themselves very early. From a letter to Mr. Kennedy: "Dear dad... I am doing my Christmas shopping Saturday with another boy. Due to fiancalinnil [spelling] difficulties at Wall Street we will not be encumbered by any weight in that direction. Woolworth's five and ten cent store will probably be our object Saturday."

The classic adult use of his understatement is the answer given to the young boy who asked how the president became a war hero. "It was very easy. They sunk my ship."

A reporter asked in early 1963: "There have been published reports that some high-placed Republican people have been making overtures to your secretary of defense [McNamara] for him to be their 1968 candidate for president. If you thought that Mr. McNamara were seriously considering these overtures, would you continue him in your cabinet?"

The president replied, "I have too high a regard for him to launch his candidacy yet."

During the early '60 campaign, he received a letter saying his brother would make a better chief executive. He replied: "I have consulted Bobby about it, and, to my dismay, the idea appeals to him."

Arthur Schlesinger writes that Kennedy's Irish background was brought out in the quizzical wit and the eruptions of boisterous humor, and that irony was the most distinctive mode of the humor: "His irony could be gentle and sharp, and it was directed at himself as often as at others." It heled him to lighten crises and to hold people and problems in balance; it was an unending source of refreshment and perspective, and an essential part of his own apparatus of self-criticism."

The president took Prime Minister Nehru of India on a costal tour of Newport on the *Honey Fitz* (family cruiser). Gliding by great mansions of a past era, Kennedy casually waved to the huge homes and said, "I wanted you to see how the average American family lives."

He was in top form at the annual dinner of Washington's Gridiron Club, an elite fraternity of Washington newsmen. "Fellow managing editors," he began. The house roared. He had been recently subjected to much criticism for cunningly managing the news. Columnist Arthur Krock had been putting the needle to Kennedy lately while Lyndon Johnson had suffered the same fate at the hands of columnist Doris Fleeson. He told Lyndon, said the president, "it was better to be Fleesonized than Krocked." Again, a roar.

He said to the National Industrial Conference Board: "It has recently been suggested that whether I serve one or two terms in the presidency,

I will find myself at the end of that period at what might be called the awkward age–too old to begin a new career and too young to write my memoirs. A similar dilemma, it seems to me, is posed by the occasion of a presidential address to a business group on business conditions less than four weeks after entering the White House. "For it is too early to be claiming credit for the new administration and too late to be blaming the old one. And it would be premature to seek your support in the next election, and inaccurate to express thanks for having had it in the last one." (*Laughter*)

William Manchester writes: "His wit is cool, merciless, and surprisingly impartial. Of course, he enjoys taunting adversaries most" as he did the businessman of the Industrial Conference Board. But no one, including relatives and closest of friends, was exempt.

Before picking up the phone to talk to Bobby Kennedy. The president turned to a guest and said, "This is the second most powerful man in the nation calling." His own brother had received the needle with that tinge of irony; that is, the irony rested in the truth of the statement.

Brother Teddy Kennedy received the same needle during the '60 campaign. Kennedy was campaigning heavily in West Virginia before the crucial primary elections of that state. The candidate being detained a bit for a particular appearance, Ted took the microphone and made a very effective speech. When the candidate arrived, he opened his remarks by saying: "I would like to tell my brother that you cannot be elected president until you are thirty-five years of age." (*Laughter*)

Bill Adler, author of *The Kennedy Wit*, writes": John F. Kennedy was a man with a keenly developed sense of humor. Few men in public life have displayed such a wit in their speeches and writings... he had the rare gift of bringing laughter to others."

In New York in the fall of 1960, both presidential candidates were invited to the Alfred E. Smith Memorial Dinner, presided over by the senior prelate of the Catholic Church in New York Cardinal Spellman.

The audience had been strongly pro-Nixon, and Kennedy was ironically entertained by the fact that the wealthy Catholics preferred a conservative Quaker, to a liberal of their own faith. Kennedy sparkled; he used the whole bag including irony, satire, and understatement to bring down the house.

> "I am glad to be here at the notable dinner once again and I am glad that Mr. Nixon is here also. [*Applause*]
>
> "Now that Cardinal Spellman has demonstrated the proper spirit, I assume that shortly I will be invited to a Quaker dinner honoring Herbert Hoover. [*Laughter*]
>
> "Cardinal Spellman is the only man so widely respected in American politics that he could bring together amicably, at the same banquet table, for the first time in this campaign, two political leaders who are increasingly apprehensive about the November election–who have long eyed each other suspiciously and who have disagreed so strongly, both publicly and privately. Vice President Nixon and Governor Rockefeller. [*Laughter*]
>
> "Mr. Nixon like the rest of us has had his troubles in this campaign. At one point even the Wall Street Journal was criticizing his tactics. That is like the *Observatore Romano* criticizing the Pope. [*Laughter*]
>
> "But I think the worst news for the Republicans this week was that Casey Stengel has been fired. It must show that perhaps experience does not count. [*Laughter and applause*]
>
> "On the matter of experience, I had announced earlier this year that if successful I would not consider campaign contributions as a substitute for experience in appointing ambassadors. Ever since I made that

statement, I have not received one single cent from my father. [*Laughter*]

"One of the inspiring notes that was struck in the last debate was struck by the vice president in his very moving warning to the children of the nation and the candidates against the use of profanity by presidents and ex-presidents when they are on the stump. And I know after fourteen years in the Congress with the vice president that he was very sincere on his views about the use of profanity. But I am told that a prominent Republican said to him yesterday in Jacksonville, Florida, 'Mr. President, that was a damn fine speech.' [*Laughter*] And the vice president said, "I appreciate the compliment but not the language.' And the Republican went on, 'Yessir, I liked it so much that I contributed a thousand dollars to your campaign.' And Mr. Nixon replied, 'The hell you say.' [*Laughter*]

"However, I would not want to give the impression that I am taking former President Truman's use of language lightly. I have sent him the following note: 'Dear Mr. President, I have noted with interest your suggestion as to where those who vote for my opponent should go. While I understand and sympathize with your deep motivation, I think it is important that our side try to refrain from raising the religious issue.;" (*Laughter and applause*)

In Los Angeles during the '60 campaign, Mr. Kennedy was facetiously asked: "Do you think a Protestant can be elected president in 1960? He retaliated, "If he's prepared to answer how he stands on the issue of separation of church and state, I see no reason why we should discriminate against him."

William Walton relates that Kennedy "was one of the great leg pullers of all times, and one of the things he adored was to make you crack up in public. During some ceremonial things, he had a great trick of rolling his eyes at you. Somebody would be making a fool of himself, you know, making a speech or something, and the president would look at you, and he wouldn't crack in the slightest."

Carlton V. Kent relates, "I remember one time, he was dedicating a dam outside of Pierce, South Dakota, the largest rolled earth dam in the world. After his speech, he notices a batch of Indians in regalia, feathers and buckskins, near the stand. He got down and went up to shake hands with them. I happened to get trapped right next to the Indians, and as he came down the line he stuck out his hand and said to me, "Hello, Chief,' and slipped right on down the line. Well, these little things tickle a man to death, and no one else notices them."

The press conferences were replete with Kennedy humor. Ted Sorensen writes that nearly all Kennedy's humorous responses were "spontaneous and both funnier and more appropriate" than any suggested ahead of time.

A reporter asked at an early press conference: "Two books have been written about you recently. One of them has been criticized as being too uncritical of you and the other, by Victor Lasky, as being too critical of you. How would you review them–if you've read them?'

The president answered: "I haven't read all of Mr. Lasky; I've just gotten the flavor of it. I see it's been highly praised by Mt. Drummond, Mr. Krock, and others. I'm looking forward to reading it, because the part that I read was not as brilliant as I gather the rest of it is from what they say about it." [*Laughter*]

During another press conference, the president received word that the United States had successfully launched a chimpanzee into space. He immediately interrupted the conference to announce the event to the assembled reporters:

"This chimpanzee who was flying in space took off at 10:08. He reports that everything is going perfectly and working well." [*Laughter*]

From a speech at the National Football Foundation Dinner: "Politics is an astonishing profession. It has enabled me to go from being an obscure member of the junior varsity at Harvard to being an honorary member of the Football Hall of Fame." [*Laughter*]

From a speech to the West Point graduates: "...I am not unmindful of the fact that two graduates of this academy have reached the White House, and neither was a member of my party.

Until I'm more certain that this trend will be broken, I wish that all of you may be generals and not commanders in chief." [*Laughter*]

From an introduction of Astronaut Alan Shepard, Jr., in a Washington ceremony honoring his space flight: "We have with us today the nation's number one television performer, who I think on last Friday morning secured the highest rating of any morning show in recent history." [*Laughter*]

Lord Harlech sums up John F. Kennedy very well: "You always felt in his presence, that life was more worth living, was greater fun." That's the way America felt; life was more fun. [*Laughter fades*]

FOUR: POTPOURRI

The tree the tempest with a crock of wood,
Throws down in front of us not to bar,
Our passage to our journey's end for good,
But just to ask us who we think we are.

Robert Frost

Strengthen all weary hands,
Steady all trembling knees,
And say to the faint hearts,
"Courage! Do not be afraid.
Look your God is coming...
He is coming to save you."

Isaiah 35:3, 4.

Presidents Kennedy and Lincoln were remarkably similar men in their traits of character. They were both men of humor (Chapter 3, *supra*). They both possessed a deep religious type of faith (Chapter 2, *supra*). They each died in frighteningly similar manners (Chapter 1, *supra*). But there were many other similarities surrounding these men, directly or indirectly.

This chapter will discuss these other similarities. The discussion is cursory by design, as I leave historical analysis to the historian. The whole book is admittedly cursory. In the area of Civil Rights, I write more detailed because of the importance of this similarity of the Lincoln-Kennedy mythology.

Each president selected a southern Democratic Senator named Johnson as his vice president. Andrew Johnson was Lincoln's second term vice president. He was preceded by Hannibal Hamlin. Each Johnson had been personally picked by Lincoln and Kennedy to give the ticket a national image. And to insure victory. Lyndon B. Johnson was from Texas. He gave balance to the ticket with the northeastern Massachusetts liberal, John F. Kennedy. Andrew Johnson was from Tennessee. Hailing from the alienated South, he too gave balance to the ticket with Lincoln of Illinois of the North.

The two Johnsons were especially tutored by Lincoln and Kennedy on the duties of the presidency. Thus, they were unusually prepared to assume command. For Lincoln and Kennedy were acutely aware of the possibility of assassination (Chapter 1, *supra*)

Both vice presidents were men of honesty and courage. They could be called typically American. For this great country has produced many such men. Their policies were continuations of their slain predecessors. But they lacked the charismatic qualities of their presidents. And the press continually impugned their dignity and wisdom. Andrew Johnson was charged with impeding Reconstruction. And Lyndon Johnson is primarily blamed for a futile land war in Southeast Asia.

Minutia similarities are as follows; Andrew Johnson was born in 1808. Lyndon Johnson was born in 1908. Both presidents were shot on Friday. Their wives each watched in horror as the bullets penetrated the back of their husbands' heads. Lincoln was elected in 1860. Kennedy was elected in 1960. Lincoln had been elected to Congress in 1846. Kennedy was elected to Congress in 1946. Andrew

Johnson died ten years after Lincoln. Lyndon Johnson died ten years after Kennedy.

Each president was assassinated by a southerner with demented, unpopular ideals. The assassins were both killed before standing trial. Conspiratorial rumor and evidence surrounded both assassinations. But history identifies John Wilkes Booth and Lee Harvey Oswald as the sole perpetrators of the deeds themselves. The name of each assassin contains fifteen letters. Kennedy and Lincoln contain seven letters; Andrew Johnson and Lyndon Johnson each contain fourteen letters. Booth shot Lincoln in a theatre and temporarily escaped through a warehouse. Oswald shot President Kennedy from a warehouse and temporarily escaped through a theatre. Lincoln had a secretary named Kennedy. Kennedy had a secretary named Lincoln. The former secretary advised Lincoln against going to Ford's theatre. The latter secretary advised Kennedy against going to Texas.

Each president was immeasurably helped in his election by a series of so-called Great Debates with his opponent. Lincoln engaged his rival, Stephen Douglas, in a series of seven debates pursuant to the 1858 senatorial campaign in Illinois. Lincoln, the Republican candidate, took an abolitionist stand. He said slavery is a "moral, a social and a political wrong." Douglas, the Democratic candidate, argued in favor of the institution of slavery. The two men debated in seven different parts of the state. As Sandburg says, "All Illinois watching, the whole country listening." The two men spoke to audiences surpassing any in past American history in size and eagerness to hear. And the whole nation patiently waited as reports of the debates were reprinted in whole or part in every newspaper in America.

Lincoln repeatedly told the citizens of Illinois: "A house divided against itself cannot stand. I believe *this government cannot endure permanently half-slave and half-free.*" While Douglas argued: "Let each state mind its own business and leave its neighbors alone!... If we will stand by that principle, then Mr. Lincoln will find that this republic can exist forever divided into free and slave states."

Prior to the Great Debates, Lincoln had scant national recognition. Douglas had considerably more. Lincoln was now suddenly thrust into national prominence. And although he lost his bid for the Senate seat, he was an instant contender for the '60 Republican presidential nomination. Lincoln had beaten Douglas in the popular vote but due to gerrymandering, Douglas held a majority of the legislature, which elected the Senator. Douglas was a contender for the Democratic nomination. Presidential candidates of their respective parties, Lincoln would defeat Douglas.

John F. Kennedy was a decided underdog to Richard M. Nixon in the 1960 presidential race. Kennedy had limited national recognition. Nixon had much more; for he had served the preceding eight years as the vice president of the United States. The candidates engaged in a series of Great Debates which would rival the Lincoln-Douglas debates. They consisted of four nationally televised debates. The whole nation this time literally watched. The "tube" made it unnecessary to await a newspaper account. Thus, we've had the Great Debates of the nineteenth and twentieth centuries unrivalled in enthusiasm and national interest by any other similar verbal duel.

The Kennedy-Nixon debates were as lively and informative as the Lincoln-Douglas counterpart. And they were the most historic since. Surveys indicated some seventy million adults watched or listened to the first debate. More than four out of five voters saw or heard at least one of the four debates. Those not seeing or listening to them, read or heard about them, just as Lincoln-Douglas.

Kennedy used short staccato sentences and rapped out his theme repeatedly: "I am not satisfied as an American with the progress that we are making... This is a great country... we can do better... *the world cannot endure half-slave and half-free.*" Nixon followed with a defensive posture: "The things that Senator Kennedy has said many of us can agree with... our disagreement is not about the goals for America but only about the means to reach those goals."

Most experts believe that the Great Debates, more than anything else, helped Kennedy defeat Nixon. Kennedy was no longer of uncertain quality. Fears of youthful inexperience and naivety were dispelled. He came across as aggressive, well informed, polished, and confident. And perhaps most importantly, the exposure greatly accelerated his campaign.

"Only events can make a president," Lincoln himself often said. The great events of the two Great Debates did much to elect Lincoln and Kennedy.

Like Lincoln, Kennedy became a winner by being a loser. Lincoln had lost the 1858 Senate bid to Douglas. After the loss he became the most sought-after speaker in the nation. And ultimately became the Republican presidential candidate of 1860. Kennedy had sought the Democratic nomination for vice president in 1956. He narrowly lost in a floor fight to Estes Kefauver. Afterwards, Kennedy became the most sought-after speaker in the nation. And ultimately became the Democratic presidential candidate of 1960.

It is certain that had Kennedy been nominated in 1956 for vice president, he would never have become president. The ticket of Stevenson and Kefauver was steamrolled by Eisenhower and Nixon. Had Kennedy been Stevenson's running mate, Kennedy would have been blamed for the loss. Party leaders would have said his Catholicism was responsible. Had Lincoln defeated Douglas in 1858, Lincoln's presidential candidacy would perhaps not have blossomed. Party leaders found Lincoln acceptable because as a non-office holder he had made few enemies. Other leading contenders at the time, such as Senator Seward and former Senator Chase, had accumulated enemies and hostility in party ranks. Lincoln would perhaps have done the same with two years' Senate experience and lost his untarnished humble image.

Both presidents became identified with the cause of Civil Rights. They became folk heroes to black America.

One of the greatest ironies of American history must be attributed to the founding fathers. That revolutionary generation which so brilliantly wrote the Declaration of Independence and the Constitution failed to see the tragic consequences of the perpetuation of slavery. The irony deserves some attention here. For along with Lincoln's efforts which preserved the Union in the face of the American Civil War and Kennedy's establishment of the Peace Corps, their respective contributions toward minority group rights, arguably is their greatest monument. That is, their contribution toward at last fulfilling the intent of the founding fathers. And making the American dream a reality for everyone.

Our founding fathers were European educated. They based the Constitution and Declaration of Independence on the great heritage of the English system of law and jurisprudence. Certain clauses were from the Magna Carta of 1215, from the Petition of Rights with which Charles I was confronted in 1628, from the English Bill of Rights of 1689 which concluded the Glorious Revolution, from the principles of John Locke, Edmund Burke, and other classical political scholars. And this proud heritage was based on the ancient theory of natural law. That is, our laws have divine sanction. The positive man-made laws come from the Creator's natural laws. And God's natural laws dictate equality among men.

The founding fathers knew this well. They said, in the Declaration of Independence, "All men are created equal."

Blackstone in his *Commentaries* declared, "This law of nature, being coeval with mankind and dictated by God Himself is of course superior in obligation to any other... no human laws are of any validity if contrary to this." Sophocles, twenty-one centuries before Blackstone, called them in the *Antigone*, "unchangeable, written laws of heaven."

The founding fathers, intimate with natural law, certainly intended "the Blessings of Liberty to ourselves and our Posterity" to include black as well as white America. But it took Lincoln and Kennedy to make the fathers' intentions clear to America. For the fathers, revolutionaries indeed, were also our first politicians. They deemed it politically expedient to remain silent on slavery.

Until Lincoln, no president, for various reasons, mostly political, really clarified these intentions. And time and events increasingly made such clarification more difficult. For the slaveholding interests had grown stronger.

During Lincoln's ascendency, the slave interests manifested much control in all three branches of government. Their fire of strength would become the fire of the Civil War. The polarization of views on slavery made extinguishment of the fire impossible.

The slave interests were so strong that none of the presidential candidates in 1860 ran on a platform of complete abolition of slavery. Including Lincoln. But he alone ran on a platform of non-extension of slave territory. The pro-slavery groups split into three parties, assuring Lincoln's election.

Lincoln, self-educated, had absorbed the principles of natural law. And he read the Bible exhaustively. To him, slavery was an unequivocal wrong. As a congressman in 1848, he introduced a bill to abolish slavery in the District of Columbia. It could never be brought to a vote. Nicolay says Lincoln was in New Orleans when he formed his first opinions on slavery: "Negroes chained, maltreated, whipped and scourged. Lincoln saw it: his heart bled; said nothing; was silent; looked bad; was thoughtful and abstracted. I can say, knowing it, that it was on this trip that he formed his opinions of slavery. It ran its iron into him then and there, May 1831. I have heard him say so often."

In 1855, writing to a friend, Joshua Speed, Lincoln said: "I confess I hate to see the poor creatures hunted down, caught, and carried back to their stripes and unrewarded toils; but I bite my lip and keep quiet."

After the Great Debates, Lincoln made his views on slavery well known throughout the length and breadth of the land. For he was a most traveled and sought-after speaker. Sandburg described those speeches: "...his lamentations over the possible outspreading of slavery had a dark music. There were listeners who couldn't help thinking and feeling he stood before them a consecrated man with a warm heart, a cool head, and he might make an able president. Lincoln defended the clause 'that all men are created equal' hundreds of times."

In late 1859, Lincoln made his famous Cooper Union speech before the moral and cultural elite of New York. Therein he made the greatest defense of the founding fathers' intent:

> "Our fathers, when they framed the Government under which we live, understood this question [of slavery] just as well, and even better, than we do now... neither the word slaves nor slavery is to be found in the Constitution, nor the word property even. The fathers called the slave a person. Their purpose was to exclude from the Constitution the idea that there could be property in man."

A reporter blurted after the speech, "He's the greatest man since St. Paul." The truth of that statement is of secondary import to the fact that Lincoln would soon be the first president to vindicate the fathers.

When Lincoln took office the only real solid Northern sentiment was for preservation of the Union. *But he would not miss his opportunity to right a wrong.* Lincoln did not have to write the Emancipation Proclamation. The attitude of much of Congress more or less conceded the continuation of slavery even after Reconstruction.

Lincoln explained to his assembled cabinet on September 22, 1862, that he was going to deliver an Emancipation Proclamation which he had been carrying around in his pocket for two months: "I determined... to issue a proclamation of emancipation... I said nothing to anyone; but I made the promise to myself and to the Maker... I have gotten you together to hear what I have written down. I do not want your advice about the main matter." Secretary of the Navy Stanton said: "It was his own act, a bold step, an executive measure originating with him."

The author of *Profiles in Courage* would perhaps ascribe these words as the reason for Lincoln's act: *"because his conscience, his personal standard of ethics, his integrity or morality–call it what you will–was stronger than the pressures of public disapproval–because his faith that his course was the best one, and would ultimately be vindicated, outweighed his fear of public reprisal."*

In November of 1864, more than 1,300,000 slaves had been freed by the Lincoln administration and the war. Now that president desired Congress to pass what he termed "the fitting if not indispensable adjunct" to his emancipation edict. In urging passage of the Thirteenth Amendment, he said in his December 1864, message, "...may we not agree that the sooner the better?" Lincoln used all his political skills and the power of the presidency in weaning the necessary votes out of Congress to insure passage.

On January 31, 1865, the amendment was passed: "Neither slavery nor involuntary servitude... shall exist within the United States, or any place subject to their jurisdiction." William Lloyd Garrison believed that Lincoln, more than any other one man, managed the parliamentary victory by which the abolition of slavery was to be made constitutional. Garrison wrote in the *Liberator*: "To whom is the country more immediately indebted for this vital and saving amendment of the Constitution than, perhaps, to any other man? –to the humble rail-splitter of Illinois–to the presidential chain-breaker for millions of the oppressed– to Abraham Lincoln!"

Ratification by two-thirds of the states did not come until after Lincoln's death. *It is an eternal monument to him.*

Legislation as far-reaching as the Thirteenth Amendment would not transpire until more than 100 years later. And it was to be approximately 100 years before another president became identified with a Civil Rights struggle. And in the process became a folk hero like Lincoln was to black Americans.

Congress passed Civil Rights Bills during Reconstruction, viz. in 1866 and 1875. They were sterile measures. Congress did not act again until 1957 and 1960 in passing Civil Rights measures. The '57 Act created a U.S. Civil Rights Commission. The '60 Act authorized Federal referees when there were patterns of discrimination in Negro voting. These were token gestures for the storm that was brewing. John Kennedy saw the clouds of the storm all over America.

The storm was black America growing restless. It had suddenly become poignantly aware of its secondary-citizen status from expanded communication media, i.e., television; from post-war prosperity, i.e., the blacks saw that the whites had it and they did not; from a heroic generation of black leaders headed by the Reverend Martin Luther King Jr.; by the catalytic effect of a milestone decision of the U.S. Supreme Court.

Black America had been impeded in its absorption into the American mainstream principally by the perpetuation of an inequitable education system. In the North and South, segregated schools prevailed. The Supreme Court had given legal sanction to Jim Crow laws by the *Plessy v. Ferguson* decision of 1896. This held that the Fourteenth Amendment did not forbid segregation of Negroes in schools (and that public facilities reserved for the colored were equal to those from which they were excluded). In other words, Constitutional sanction was given the "separate-but-equal doctrine". In 1954, the Supreme Court decision held that separate educational facilities are inherently unequal in

Brown v. Board of Education of Topeka which overturned Plessy. This decision and Dr. King's efforts sparked a revolution which continues to date. King and the blacks found an ally in the most strategic and important position in the world. President Kennedy upon his ascendency joined their revolution. He did not have to. It was politically dangerous. *But he would not miss his chance to right a wrong.*

When Kennedy took office, southern leaders still had certain strangleholds on the U.S. Government (Chapter One, *supra.*). Their grip was in some ways as strong as in Lincoln's day. For the executive and legislative branches had been unable to ameliorate the suppression of black America since Lincoln's tenure.

Now the fathers' dream must be fulfilled for all. The activists of the black South fortunately followed the non-violent Martin Luther King. King had borrowed the tactics of Gandhi which had won independence for India. King schooled his people to demonstrate non-violently and patiently, starting with a bus boycott in Montgomery, Alabama. The demonstrations spread to many cities. The sit-in phase began in 1960 at lunch counters and drug stores. Presently, the agitation spread to Northern cities in the black man's search for better schools, housing, services, and status. The Jim Crow philosophy was being challenged by peaceful revolution for economic and political rights.

As the presidential election campaign of 1960 began, both parties adopted Civil Rights planks in their respective platforms. Neither candidate enjoyed a clear advantage over the other among black voters. Nixon was just so much better known than Kennedy. Then came the debates. And the campaign picked up steam. Kennedy was scrutinized by black America, and they liked what they saw and heard. Sorenson writes that "Kennedy was so clearly free from any prejudice or stereotyped response and impression." He did not use hollow rhetoric. He would boldly say that he favored freedom riders and sit-in protests. No other national leader would or did so speak. His personality gave black voters a natural affinity for him. His courage and honesty came across. Furthermore, here was a minority citizen, an Irish Roman Catholic, running for president.

Could this be a spectrum of Lincoln? Would this man at long last fulfill the fathers' intent and dream?

In April of 1959, Kennedy gave a speech on Civil Liberties in Washington, D.C., at the annual conference of the Clearing House. Therein, he indicated his deep belief in the tenets of the founding fathers:

> "The authors of the Constitution made clear their own belief that self-government on the one hand, and the truth on the other hand that all men are created equal and endowed by their Creator with certain inalienable rights are in fact two sides of the same coin."

During the campaign, Dr. King was jailed on a minor traffic charge. A designed concoction by local Southern officials to suppress the "black troublemaker". John Kennedy phoned Mrs. King, expressing sympathy. He dispatched brother Bob Kennedy to call the authorities and effect King's release. News of this move spread like wildfire over the underground press of black America. The affinity for JFK turned into a love affair of complete trust. And Kennedy subsequently received an overwhelming majority of the black votes. The majority of whites, almost predictably, proceeded to vote against Kennedy.

The Negro's hopes and trust in Kennedy were honored. He began fulfilling the dream on the day of his inauguration. As the Coast Guard Academy's representative company marched past his Pennsylvania Avenue reviewing stand in the inaugural parade, the president detected an absence of black faces. He immediately, from his glassed-in box, phoned an executive order calling for recruitment and increased enrollment of blacks at the academy. This was the first of many such executive commands. Kennedy appointed and promoted Negro officials, judges, White House aides, and ambassadors.

Kennedy interpreted the 1957 and 1960 Civil Rights Acts to mean that his attorney general had the *responsibility*–not just the *authority*–to investigate and to bring legal action where citizens are denied the right to register and vote on account of race. He had worked vigorously for passage of these acts while in the U.S. Senate. The day after Robert Kennedy was confirmed as attorney general by the Senate, the president gave his brother and the Civil Rights Division of the Department of Justice standing orders; *"Get the road maps and go."* They had begun, by December of 1961, investigations in sixty-one Southern counties. A suit was filed against the whole state of Mississippi. They began to cut the heart out of the racial status quo of the South. And they were doing it with those watered-down Civil Rights Act of '57 and '60.

The *Brown* decision and Supreme Court decisions on interstate commerce were implemented by non-discriminatory use of Federal funds. He employed Federal troops to assure admittance of blacks in several schools. Most notably, the state universities of Mississippi and Alabama. By executive orders, he ended all discriminatory practices within all Federal agencies and government institutions.

President Kennedy and Civil Rights leaders knew that a comprehensive Civil Rights Bill was needed. Vindication at last for the fathers! Congress was hostile. They rejected the bill he sent to them in February of 1963. Indicative of the congressional mood and Southern control thereof (Chapter One, *supra.*) was their action re HUD. Kennedy had proposed the establishment of the Department of Housing and Urban Development, but Congress rejected it because word had leaked that Kennedy intended to appoint a black secretary to fill the new cabinet office. And Congress felt the tremors of a white-constituent backlash when Kennedy made typical bold remarks such as: "We owe a debt of gratitude to the Negro in the streets for calling attention to the American dream."

Kennedy was tuned in to the dream. He pitched his tent for battle. Lincoln had told his Congress: "The dogmas of the past are inadequate for the stormy present. We must think anew, we must act anew, we must disenthrall ourselves." One hundred years later, Kennedy was now telling his Congress: "In this year of the Emancipation Centennial, justice requires us to insure the blessings of liberty for all Americans and their posterity–not merely for reasons of economic efficiency, world diplomacy, and domestic tranquility–but, above all, because it is right."

Why was President Kennedy wearing his armor and waving his sword in the front ranks of this revolution? *"Because his conscience, his personal standard of ethics, his integrity or morality–call it what you will–was stronger than the pressures of public disapproval–because his faith that his course was the best one, and would ultimately be vindicated, outweighed his fear of public reprisal."*

He took to television in June of '63: "We are confronted primarily by a moral issue. It is as old as the scriptures and is as clear as the American Constitution." The fathers smiled cherubic smiles from above. "It ought to be possible for every American to enjoy the privileges of being American without regard to race or color . to treat our fellow Americans as we want to be treated... This nation, for all its hopes and boasts, will not be fully free until all its citizens are free".

The president was into scripture. Kennedy's speeches, like Lincoln's, has a biblical ring. Not a bloody hellfire pulpit style. They intelligently employed scripture and its lessons. They contemporized natural law to the nation's plight. This was their faith, their source of courage.

Kennedy now needed both courage and Lincoln's parliamentary skill to get his Civil Rights bill through an unwilling Congress. By August, his efforts were still unrequited. Two hundred thousand people led by King marched on Washington. Their demonstrations called for immediate passage of the bill and equal rights for all, forever, once and for all. King told the crowd: "I have a dream." Kennedy told King, "I too have a dream."

The strongest Civil Rights vehicle since the Emancipation Proclamation, the embodiment of the dream, the vindication of the fathers, passed only after Kennedy's death. *It is an eternal monument to him.*

Harry Golden writes: "The cruel truth and even more cruel coincidence is that our two Emancipator Presidents were assassinated within one century of each other before the fruits of their struggle were realized... But at least history gave us these men and perhaps we, as a nation, may one day measure collectively to what they measured alone."

President Kennedy enjoyed an advantage over President Lincoln in the perpetuation of his folk hero/legend status. His brother Robert survived him. He was John in looks, voice, mannerisms. Those who subscribed to the legend looked to Robert to complete John's unfinished work.

After Martin Luther King's assassination, riots marked almost every American black ghetto. Bobby was probably the one white in America who could safely walk through a black ghetto during this burning, smoldering crisis. (Mayor John Lindsay of New York was a possible exception as well). He spoke in one such ghetto on the evening of King's assassination. And he was speaking publicly now for the first time of his brother John's assassination: "...my brother was killed too by a white man... what we need in the United States is... a feeling of justice towards those who still suffer within our country, whether they be white or they be black."

And the black underground telegraphed Bobby's words. Like the call to King's wife, eight years earlier, Bobby's speech spread as fast as the fires. It spread the sharing and identification of grief. The transformation was now complete. Kennedy was a black man in white skin.

He was the only white man invited to the Moorhead College eulogy podium of King's funeral. Bobby received more than 90 percent of the black votes in all the presidential primaries in the spring of 1968.

Spring would never turn to summer for Senator Kennedy. The fire of hope had also been burning brightly within the hearth fires of all minority America: the poor of Appalachia; Cesar Chavez's Mexican American grape pickers; the reservation Indians; urban white immigrants; and above all, the restless, rebellious, alienated youth of America. With Bobby's own tragic slaying, the fire of hopeful conciliation among all of America's peoples, young and old, black and white, rich and poor, was doused. But the fire of the myth of the brothers Kennedy blazed ever brighter. As well as that of Lincoln, with every tragic assassination of the 1960s.

AFTERWORD

History has made Lincoln and Kennedy complete legends. But the real legend is that they were human indeed, flesh and blood, not marble statues, not supernatural saints. They were less frail than most of us. Their natural human frailty was subdued by courage with its wellspring of faith. They each had a fine sense of humor and humility. And this gave them colored imagination and good judgment. It was only time and events which made them legends.

Webster defines legend as "a story coming down from the past; esp. one popularly accepted as historical though not verifiable". The Lincoln legend. A poor, humble rail-splitter, who was born and reared in a log cabin. He grew up to be president, but he remained a simple man. He was honest, kind, and good. He saved the Union and freed the slaves. His words and deeds became like scripture. He was ordained Saint Abe after his martyrdom. The Kennedy legend. A dashing, handsome young man, he was trained and tutored by his parents and great teachers to someday lead his people. He heroically served his country in warfare. He then continued his apprenticeship of youth in Congress before becoming president. His words and deeds became like scripture. He was ordained Saint John after his martyrdom.

Lincoln and Kennedy pose sternly on millions of coins. Parks, schools, streets and even whole towns bear their names. Lincoln is more a historical person than Kennedy, though no less the legend, simply because he has been dead for more than one hundred fifty years. Also, Kennedy left many kin bearing his name, not the least being his youngest brother Edward, a United States Senator, and to many, he was the heir-apparent to the martyred Jack and also Bobby. (Teddy was driving toward the presidency until he drove off the Chappaquiddick bridge). So, where the Lincoln legend needs national holidays and shrines to perpetuate itself, the Kennedy legend has living reminders to add to the already too many shrines. Robert Kennedy, Jr. is running for president at this writing.

Many unfortunately remember Kennedy and Lincoln only because they can hardly avoid traveling Kennedy Highway to Lincoln Park. Some remember them for their deeds and like or dislike them accordingly. The bright historians and political analysts have done very thorough dissecting jobs on the deeds of Kennedy and Lincoln. Kennedy has been termed everything from a wise and bold leader to a blunderer. Lincoln, everything from genius to buffoon. Suffice it to say, neither lived long enough to do all he wanted to do.

Many simply loved these men for what they were. More important than deeds, these men moved people. Those who so loved them were moved. This is the great Kennedy and Lincoln shrine.

They both received great support and love from minority groups, because of their respective contributions to minority causes, essentially to black America. But Kennedy mostly touched and moved the young. The young who knew no color or creed differentiation, and who accepted him for what he was. And Lincoln mostly moved middle America who were tired of war, who lived in small communities and farms. The average American who knew Lincoln was not a big-city lawyer or industrialist or newspaper editor, but simply one of them. They trusted Lincoln. The young, trusted Kennedy.

Lincoln tried to make the American people the leaders of an awakening of plain people the world over. For he was plain. Kennedy tried to make the American people the leaders of an awakening of young people the world over. For he was young. Historians can hardly deny their success. But it was the catharsis of martyrdom which climaxed Kennedy's appeal to the young and made them more politically motivated than ever before in our nation's history. Ditto Lincoln and middle America. Both men polarized emotions. Few simply liked or disliked them. More hated or loved them. As said, much of the love for Kennedy was from young America, and for Lincoln, from plain America. The hate at the other end of the pole was so strong it almost predictably had to kill them. If you loved them, you understand that in the last analysis, they were simply good and decent men who saw wrong and tried to right it, saw war and tried to stop it, saw suffering and tried to heal it. And I was among the young people of America awakened by Kennedy.

BIBLIOGRAPHICAL ACKNOWLEDGMENTS

Adler, Bill. *The Kennedy Wit.* New York: Citadel Press, 1964.

——*More Kennedy Wit.* New York: Citadel Press, 1964

Arnold, Isaac Newton. *History of Abraham Lincoln and the Overthrow of Slavery.* Chicago: Clarke & Co., 1866.

—— *Life of Abraham Lincoln.* Chicago: Fergus Printing Co., 1885.

Barton, William E. *The Soul of Abraham Lincoln.* Indianapolis: Bobs-Merrill Co., 1927.

Bishop, James A. *A Day in the Life of President Kennedy.* New York: Random House, 1964.

—— *The Day Kennedy Was Shot.* New York: Funk and Wagnalls, 1968.

—— *The Day Lincoln Was Shot.* New York: Harper and Row, 1955.

Bowen, Catherine Drinker. *Miracle at Philadelphia.* Boston, Toronto. Little, Brown & Company, 1966.

Brockett, L.P. *Life and Times of Abraham Lincoln.* Philadelphia: Bradley & Co., 1865.

Brooks, Noah. *Abraham Lincoln and the Downfall of Slavery.* New York: G.P. Putnam & Sons, 1894.

Browne, Francis F. *The Everyday Life of Abraham Lincoln*. Chicago: Browne & Howell Co., 1913.

Burns, James MacGregor. *John Fitzgerald Kennedy: A Political Profile*. New York: Harcourt, Brace & World, 1961.

Case, Carlton Britton. *Wit and Humor of Abraham Lincoln*. Chicago: Shrewsbury Publishing Co., 1924.

Charnswood, Lord. *Abraham Lincoln*. New York: Henry Holt & Co., 1917.

Cushing, Richard Cardinal. *JFK Memorial Book*. *Look* magazine. Cowled Magazines (USA), 1964.

Dineen, Joseph Francis. *The Kennedy Family*. Boston: Little, Brown & Co., 1960.

Fay, Paul B., Jr. *The Pleasure of His Company*. New York: Harper & Row, 1966.

Fox, Gresham George. *Abraham Lincoln's Religion*. New York: Exposition Press, 1959.

Golden, Harry Lewis. *Mr. Kennedy and the Negroes*. Cleveland: World Publishing Co., 1964.

Herndon, Bouton. *Humor of JFK*. Greenwich, Conn.: Fawcett Publications, 1964.

Herndon, William Henry. *Life of Lincoln*. New Yor: A & C Boni, 1930.

Hertz, Emanuel. *Abraham Lincoln*. New York: American Hebrew Publishing Co., 1927.

Kennedy, John Fitzgerald. *The Burden and the Glory*. Edited by Allan Nevins. New York, London, Evanston: Harper & Row, Publishers, 1955, 1960, 1962, 1964.

———— *Profiles in Courage. The Strategy of Peace*. Edited by Allan Nevins.

———— *To Turn the Tide*. Edited by John W. Garner.

———— *Why England Slept*. New York: W. Funk, Inc., 1945.

King, Martin Luther, Jr. "*JFK Memorial Book. Look* magazine, Cowles Magazines (USA), 1964.

Lamon, Ward Hill. *Life of Abraham Lincoln.* Boston: J. P. Osgood & Co., 1872.

Lincoln, Evelyn. *My Twelve Years with JFK.* New York: D. McKay Co., 1965.

Manchester, William. *Portrait of a President.* Boston-Toronto: Little, Brown & Company, 1962.

—— *Death of a President.* New York, Evanston, London: Harper and Row Publishers, 1964.

McClure, J. B. *Anecdotes of Abraham Lincoln.* Chicago: American News Co., 1867.

McEvoy, Kevin. *Two Kennedys.* Glen Rock, New Jersey: Paulist Press, 1969.

McCarthy, Joe. *The Remarkable Kennedys.* New York: Dial Press, 1960.

McNamara, Robert. *JFK Memorial Book. Look* magazine, Cowles Magazines (USA), 1964.

Morrison, Samuel Eliot. *Oxford History of the American People.* New York: Oxford University Press, 1965.

Nevins, Allan. *The Emergence of Lincoln.* New York Scribner, 1950.

Nicolay, John G., and John Hay. *Complete Works of Abraham Lincoln.* New York: They Century Company, 1894.

—— *Abraham Lincoln: A History.* New York: F.D. Taredy Co., 1905.

Salinger, Pierre, and Sander Vanocur. *A Tribute to John F. Kennedy.* Chicago: Encyclopedia Britannica, Inc., 1964.

Sandburg, Carl. *The Prairie Years. The War Years.* New York: Harcourt, Brace and Company, Inc., 1936.

Schlesinger, Arthur M., Jr. *A Thousand Days.* Boston: Houghton-Mifflin Company, 1965.

Settle, T. J. *The Wisdom of JFK. The Faith of JFK.* Introduction by Richard Cardinal Cushing New York: E. P. Dutton & Co., Inc. 1965.

Sidey, Hugh. *John F. Kennedy: President.* New Yor: Atheneum, 1964.

Sorenson, Theodore C. *Kennedy.* New York: Harper & Row Publishers, 1965.

———— *The Kennedy Legacy*. New York: The Macmillan Company, 1969

Taggart, David Raymond. *The Faith of Abraham Lincoln*. Topeka, Kansas: The Service Print Shop, 1943.

Warren Commission on the Assassination of President Kennedy, Report of the. New York, London, Toronto: McGraw-Hill, 1964.

White, Theodore H. *The Making of the President: 1960*. New York: Atheneum House, Inc. 1961.

Wicker, Tom. *Kennedy Without Tears: The Man Beneath the Myth*. New York: William Morrow & Company, 1964.

Wordsworth, R. D. *Abe Lincoln's Anecdotes and Stories*. Boston: The Mutual Book Co., 1960.

THE AUTHOR

Darrell Russell is a retired judge of the District Court of Maryland. He now practices law at a reduced pace in a small firm in eastern Baltimore County. He lives in Towson, Maryland. Three of his four adult children are nearby. His fourth child, Maureen, resides in Birmingham Alabama, where she runs marathons like her dad. She obtained her graduate degree from South Alabama. Her brother Brendan also went to Alabama at the Tuscaloosa campus. Roll Tide Roll! Judge Russell's other two children, Graham and Eileen, served their country in the Navy (SEAL program) and AmeriCorps, respectively. Russell spent early years as a lacrosse, tennis and cross-country coach at his alma mater, Loyola University Maryland. He was the first commissioner of the National Lacrosse League. He has authored several books on law and sports, his dual avocations. He is a trustee of his Elks Lodge in Towson.

Lincoln and Kennedy Redux was first written by Judge Russell while a law student at the University of Baltimore. It was entitled *Lincoln and Kennedy: Looked at Kindly Together*. He has redone it out of nostalgia for the halcyon Kennedy days of Camelot.